A Labyrinth Prayer Handbook

A Labyrinth Prayer Handbook

Creative resources for worship and reflection

Sally Welch

CANTERBURY
PRESS
Norwich

© Sally Welch 2014

First published in 2014 by the Canterbury Press Norwich
Editorial office
3rd Floor, Invicta House,
108–114 Golden Lane,
London EC1Y 0TG

Canterbury Press is an imprint of Hymns Ancient & Modern Ltd
(a registered charity)
13A Hellesdon Park Road, Norwich,
Norfolk NR6 5DR, UK

www.canterburypress.co.uk

Scripture quotations are from
The New International Version (NIV) copyright © 1973, 1978, 1984 by
International Bible Society. Used by permission of Hodder & Stoughton
Ltd, a member of the Hodder Headline Ltd.
The New Revised Standard Version of the Bible (NRSV) copyright 1989
by the Division of Christian Education of the National Council of the
Churches of Christ in the USA. Used by permission. All rights reserved.
The Voice Bible copyright © 2012 Thomas Nelson, Inc.

Prayers from *Common Worship: Services and Prayers for the Church of
England* (2000), *Common Worship Daily Prayer* (2005) and *Common
Worship: Times and Seasons* (2006) are copyright © The Archbishops'
Council and are reproduced by permission.

British Library Cataloguing in Publication data

A catalogue record for this book is available
from the British Library

978 1 84825 672 9

Typeset by Regent Typesetting
Printed and bound in Great Britain by
CPI Group (UK) Ltd, Croydon

Contents

[v]

With grateful thanks to John and Pat Barker,
without whom the journey could not have
been made.

To Binka, who knows a lot about labyrinths.

Introduction

Encounters with Labyrinths

My experience of labyrinths is as roundabout and deceptively meandering as walking the labyrinth itself. As a newly ordained priest, I quickly discovered that in order to maintain my relationship with God in the face of so many demands upon my time and energies, I had to put aside some time regularly to reflect and pray. Being a very active person, I had always found sitting still to pray or meditate very challenging and draining rather than energizing, and had thus arrived at pilgrimage as the ideal way for me to sustain my spiritual life. Pilgrimage, a spiritual journey to a sacred place, finds its roots in the biblical journeys of the Old and New Testaments, and has played a major part in Christian prayer traditions ever since, reaching a peak in medieval times and recently enjoying a revival among contemporary Christians. Thus, engaged with exploring the spirituality of pilgrimage, I journeyed throughout England and Europe, meeting God in the landscape and people I encountered, and experiencing some profoundly moving moments.

However, for a priest with a parish and family, pilgrimage is not always easily accessible, and so I began to search for a similar method of praying that was available to me more readily. In my research on the history of pilgrimage I had learnt that when travelling through Europe had become too difficult and dangerous even for the most adventurous of medieval pilgrims, labyrinths had been built into the floors of many of the great cathedrals, possibly as a symbolic substitute for a lengthier and more hazardous expedition. The most famous surviving example of these great works is the labyrinth set into the floor of Chartres Cathedral, and I duly visited the cathedral in order to walk the labyrinth myself. To my disappointment, I discovered that the nave, where the labyrinth is situated, was covered with rows of chairs, and that walking the labyrinth was only possible on Fridays between Lent and All Saints. Undeterred, I travelled to Amiens Cathedral, where a replica of an earlier labyrinth is to be found in one of the side aisles. At last I was able to walk the labyrinth, with my whole family, on a very cold New Year's Eve.

Reflecting on this walk, I discovered that I had learnt two things – first, that if I tried to look ahead to see where the path led, I would stumble and lose the path I was walking on, and second, that my family, although they were all walking at different speeds and were at different places on the labyrinth pathway, were all held by the same path, in the same space. Developing these reflections, I understood the need for greater awareness of the moment, for a focus not always on the things of tomorrow, but on the events and people held in the present. I also felt great gratitude for the way in which we are all held together, bound by love for each other and for God in a way that also enables difference.

Returning to my parish, I determined to share this experience with my parishioners and others, and with the help of the Diocese of Oxford I became the keeper of a 24'/7.3m canvas labyrinth in the Chartres style. Since then, I have travelled around the country, talking about labyrinths as a way of prayer, and encouraging others to share the experience of walking the labyrinth. This book is a result of these travels, and encounters with others who have walked the same path in similar and in very different contexts. It is designed to help those who already have some experience of labyrinth spirituality to explore it further, as well as to enable those who are new to this way of praying to benefit from their experience.

I

A Brief History of Labyrinths

In essence, a labyrinth is a single pathway, turning and curving upon itself in a complex pattern around a central point. If the walker begins at the entrance to the labyrinth and follows the path faithfully, they will always arrive at the centre. From there, the same, unique path will be followed in order to arrive outside the labyrinth once more.

It is important to stress that a labyrinth is not a maze. A maze is a pattern that offers more than one path, of which only one leads to the centre point – the other paths are misleading and finish in dead ends. A maze is for getting lost in; a labyrinth is for realizing that we are never truly lost, but can always find ourselves in God. There are no dead ends or wrong turnings in a labyrinth, simply the one path that will always lead us to the centre and safely out again.

It is believed that the labyrinth pattern is an archetype; that is, a constantly recurring symbol that can be found in the environment that surrounds us – in the patterns of a seashell, the whorls of our fingerprints, the movements of winds and tides. Some believe that the labyrinth pattern is also a human psychological archetype – for evidence of labyrinth patterns and various myths accompanying these patterns can be found in most major civilizations across the continents and down through history. Examples of labyrinths date from ancient Egyptian times and encompass the Hopi Indians' 'man in a maze', Celtic and even Chinese examples.

The earliest Christian labyrinth is said to date from the fourth century AD and is set in the doorway of an Algerian church. Small finger labyrinths were certainly in evidence before the evolution of an architecture that could span large spaces enabled the development of size-able floor labyrinths such as the example in Chartres Cathedral. Indeed, there is evidence that many of the great European cathedrals, including those at Sens, Arras, Reims, Amiens, Bayeux and Poitiers, possessed either floor or wall labyrinths dating from late medieval times. This period coincided with the heyday of pilgrimage, with pilgrims forming a network of routes and communica-tions throughout Europe and the Middle East as they journeyed to Santiago de Compostela, Rome, Jerusalem and many other lesser pilgrimage sites. It is from this coincidence that the relationship between labyrinth and pilgrimage has been suggested, and it seems to be highly logical that a symbolic pilgrimage should be made avail-able for those unable to make the entire journey.

Sadly, although these labyrinths remained in place for hundreds of years, most of them had been destroyed by the early years of the nineteenth century. This may have been as a result of a change in the way of thinking brought about by the Reformation and the Enlightenment, when an approach to reality based on cause and effect, with a direct line linking the two and concentrated on the material things of this world, replaced a more discursive, experiential reality focused on eternity. A science-based way of thinking would have no need for a wandering, circular way of praying, preferring a more direct route to the Creator.

Today, we are returning once more to a network-based mind set. Our realities are to be found not in the things we can see or touch but in computer networks spanning the globe. Relationships are possible not just with those people we can talk to or hear, but with those we may never see, living many miles away from us, but drawn closer through networks of communications that weave complex patterns through an invisible world. Once again we need to release our right-brain creativity from the constraints of the left-brain paradigm of logic and process, enabling both sides to work together in harmony for a holistic approach to faith and human existence. The action of setting forth on a journey with a destination that we can only trust we will arrive at, rather than looking ahead in certainty to a clearly marked point, sets us free to journey in our hearts and minds to places that cannot be reached by rational thought. The simple action of walking, of treading a single pathway, occupies the restless striving of our human nature with its perpetual need to get ahead, to make progress. In turn, this enables us to find the peace that might otherwise escape us in the busyness of our everyday lives, and the space to encounter God through the metaphor of our journey upon the labyrinth.

Critics of the labyrinth as a pathway to prayer might assert that there is no biblical foundation for such a pattern of ritual walking, which might indeed seem true – the labyrinth is not mentioned in either the Old or New Testaments. However, a meditative journeying in a concentrated space, time spent in a liminal place, enabling growth and transformation to take place, is a fundamental metaphor in the Bible. The Sinai Desert, through which Moses and his people journeyed, crossing and re-crossing a space that takes only a fraction of that time to journey through physically, but which occupied 40 years of Old Testament experience, while the refugees from Egypt learned what it was to be the Children of Israel, is a powerful labyrinth metaphor. So too is the claustrophobic geography of Jesus' ministry, intense in its place and duration, world-changing in its effect.

The labyrinth is, after all, simply a pattern in the ground, and we would be wise to remember that before we credit it with more powers than it should possess. However, as part of a toolkit for the Christian spiritual life, enabling transformation and change, encouraging a deepening relationship with God, offering a safe place for moments of personal insight and revelation, the labyrinth can be an exciting, challenging and satisfying prayer experience from which we could all learn.

2

Planning a Labyrinth Event

Although introducing the way of prayer and meditation that is the labyrinth may seem at the outset a relatively simple operation, it can be a lengthy and time-consuming business, especially if the audience is not used to the concept. Different amounts of preparation are needed for different events – a workshop, lecture or worship event will need less time than a series of workshops or the introduction of a permanent labyrinth, but even the briefest of ventures will need thought and preparation.

Running a labyrinth workshop, whether it is for half a day or a whole day, or simply leading a labyrinth walk, is a valuable undertaking but one that should not be underestimated in terms of the time and effort required to ensure that everything runs smoothly. Preparations should be made well in advance so that when the time for the event arrives, you are calm, in control and able to focus on the requirements of those attending the workshop. The following are some factors that you might want to take into consideration as you plan your labyrinth event.

Getting people on board

Introducing a labyrinth to a group that is new to the idea should be done with great care and consideration. If you are concerned only with leading a workshop or offering a service of worship, there is less to be done in terms of preparation, as very often you will have been invited into the venue by people who are already on board with the idea. However, it is always wise to check that the leaders of the organization involved are comfortable with what you are proposing – it can be a good idea to send a booklet or leaflet outlining the nature and purpose of a labyrinth so that the leaders are briefed if they in their turn are challenged.

Choosing a theme

If you are running a workshop, the theme of the workshop and its situation are often tied in very closely together, with the topic suggested by the location, and vice versa. For example, a small labyrinth built out of stones on a beach might inspire workshops that focus on creation and the environment, perhaps with an emphasis on our role in caring for our surroundings, or the way in which human beings are an integral part of the whole of God's creation, every atom of which carries the divine spark of God's love. Again, a church setting at the beginning of Advent might be a suitable venue for a workshop on light, reflecting on Jesus as the Light of the World, perhaps including a candlelit labyrinth walk. Alternatively a workshop in a hall or retreat centre at this time could be based around the concept of waiting, of allowing God the time and space to work within us and through us.

If you have been asked to lead an event by an external organization, they may suggest a theme to you – for example, a PCC may ask for one that explores vocation or stewardship, or a women's group for one that channels creativity and enables personal expression. If you do not feel the theme is suitable or easily adaptable for the location or the labyrinth, then it is best to offer alternatives rather than struggle on with something that may prove ultimately unsatisfactory. For many people, coming to the labyrinth for the first time, a simple theme on a familiar topic might be most appropriate, as the familiar offers an unthreatening stepping-off point for a new experience that it is hoped will, in its turn, shed a different light on a well-known topic.

Most importantly, make sure that the topic that has been decided on is one that you are comfortable with and secure in. This does not mean that you should not explore new ways of working with the labyrinth or continue to add new themes to your workshop menu, simply that preparation and studying beforehand needs to be thorough enough that at the time of the workshop itself you are confident in your topic, as relaxed as possible, and able to focus your attention on those who are attending the workshop.

Location

As has already been stated, this is often suggested by, or suggests, the theme. This interdependence means that knowledge of the location is very useful when planning a workshop. You may have been asked to take a portable labyrinth to a specific location such as a school or retreat centre, or the venue may already have one of its own. Either way, it is helpful to have some idea of the place beforehand. If it is possible to visit the venue before the workshop, this is obviously the best way of gaining information, but a look at the venue's website will often be very helpful, and a conversation with the onsite co-ordinator should fill in any gaps in your information.

It is useful to know, for example, how open the labyrinth will be to others not participating in the workshop. A labyrinth that is set in a relatively public place, allowing walkers to be observed, will produce a different atmosphere from one that is in a closed space. When planning a workshop or walk in a church or chapel, for example, it helps to find out whether it will be open to visitors or not. If the venue is in a school, college or other institution, it is useful to know how much observation the walkers will be under. One labyrinth walk I know of in a school could have been a disaster when it transpired that the entire school would be walking on their way to lunch directly past the room in which the labyrinth was laid out. Fortunately, some hasty rearranging of the programme timetable meant that this potentially embarrassing experience for the young walkers could be avoided.

Using the labyrinth

If you are leading a workshop with a labyrinth that you are familiar with, the potential for problems is far less. However, it is critical to make sure that the dimensions of the labyrinth you are bringing with you, or are planning to create at the venue, are suitable for the location. Very often people will misjudge the size of their venue, believing it to be larger than it is, and on more than one occasion I have arrived somewhere with a canvas labyrinth to a space that could indeed fit in an object

24'/7.3m in diameter, were it not for the pillar or tent pole right in the middle!

I was once asked to lead a labyrinth quiet day at a retreat centre that had its own labyrinth. I duly sent in my proposed programme, which I had constructed with the idea that the labyrinth would be about 24'/7.3m in diameter, which is a fairly standard size for labyrinths. Ones of this size can be walked in about half an hour, so I had planned for three walks, each following a short reflection. The centre leader emailed back to say that their labyrinth was in fact an exact copy of the Chartres labyrinth – 42'/12.8m in diameter – and consequently took about an hour to walk! I had to re-plan the programme, but was grateful that I had been alerted to this and was not forced to make hasty changes on my arrival at the centre!

Equipment

As I have led more and more labyrinth events, so the list of equipment that I take with me has grown in length. A more in-depth discussion of the particular needs of individual environments follows, but there are some items that should always be carried.

If the labyrinth is a portable canvas one, then a notice asking people to refrain from eating or drinking on the labyrinth is vital. So too is one that requests the removal of shoes for all but those needing to wear them for medical reasons. This is simply good housekeeping, and no one objects. It is, however, quite useful if you can remind people that they will be walking shoeless in any information about the event you send out in advance – I have witnessed the embarrassment of many people whose holey socks have been revealed to the rest of the group!

A short, introductory notice or leaflet that gives simple instructions for walkers, such as the etiquette of sharing a path with others and the reassurance that they cannot get lost, is also a good idea. This will act not only as a reminder to those on the walk, but to inform onlookers who might be curious as to what is going on. The leaflet might contain these words or similar:

> The labyrinth has a long established spiritual history, with the medieval labyrinths of the great French cathedrals such as Chartres, Rouen and Amiens being used as a central focus for prayer and worship. Today it is again being seen as offering an opportunity for reflection, renewal and spiritual growth.
>
> The labyrinth has only one route, so there are no tricks to it and no dead ends. It has a single circuitous path that winds into the centre. The person walking it uses the same path to return and the entrance then becomes the exit. The path is in full view, which allows a person to be quiet and focus internally.
>
> Many have found that walking a labyrinth can be a powerful spiritual experience, enabling people to engage in or deepen their relationship with God. With no 'right' or 'wrong' way to walk it, nothing that 'has to be done', its flexibility and accessibility enable people to engage with God in a direct and personal way. Walking with a group of people is an experience of community, of all being on the same path, which gives a first taste of the concept of the community of the Church.

Guidelines for the walk

Walking the labyrinth may be seen as a three-stage reflection. First, as the labyrinth is entered, there is the opening of mind and heart to what God might want to say. On arrival at the centre of it, time can be taken for reflection. Finally, there is the journeying outwards with insights gained.

Practical notes

To enable freedom of movement, leave an interval of time and space between walkers.

On entering the labyrinth, the mind should be quietened, and the body stilled; every movement, every breath, should be made deliberate.

It is important to find a pace that is comfortable, whether brisk or slow. Other walkers on the path can be overtaken or not. Don't forget that the path is two-way; some will be journeying outwards as others journey in.

When the centre is reached, there is an opportunity for reflection before following the same path out.

There are as many different ways to walk the labyrinth as there are people that walk it, and each person will discover something new.

It is a good idea to provide some paper and pens or coloured pencils so that walkers can journal or illustrate their experiences on the labyrinth. A large box of tissues will prove useful, as some walkers can find the event quite emotional. If you are keen to remind walkers to take off their shoes before walking, bring a spare pair with you to place at the entrance to the labyrinth – it will prove a more effective sign than a written notice.

Extra items needed for themed or seasonal labyrinth events are included in the outlines that follow in later chapters.

Before you begin

If the labyrinth event is in a venue that is not your own, or not one familiar to you, arrive in plenty of time to organize the space so that you feel comfortable in it before welcoming your workshop or lecture participants. Setting up a labyrinth takes time and energy, whether it is drawing one out on the floor or unfolding a canvas one or simply familiarizing yourself with one that is already in place. If you are able, it is a good idea to walk the labyrinth yourself – this will not only calm you and help you to centre before the event itself, but it will familiarize you with any potential pitfalls such as uneven ground, tight corners or uncomfortable patches. Make sure your notices are in place, that the paper and pens are to hand, and the box of tissues in a visible, accessible place. If the labyrinth requires shoes to be removed, either remove your own and place them by the entrance, or use those you brought with you for this purpose.

At the end

After the event, it is important that you allow enough time for those who did not feel able to contribute to a plenary session to have conversations and discussions with you in a more personal way. Do not rush to pack up your labyrinth – there may be people who wish to walk it again in solitude. Try not to sweep everything up and away immediately as this will break the meditative mood that has hopefully been created, and may prevent emotional closure for some people. In some cases, the clearing away of the labyrinth and the tidying of the space can become part of the ritual, as participants return from the liminal space created and rejoin their everyday lives and preoccupations.

3

Ideas and Outlines for Themed Workshops or Quiet Days

General guidelines

One of the most popular ways of experiencing the labyrinth is through a workshop, offered by churches, retreat centres or other institutions. These can be very rewarding for the participants as they offer a fairly in-depth encounter, and often more than one opportunity to walk the labyrinth. Workshops are a significant undertaking for the leader, and each one needs to be carefully adjusted to suit the needs of the people attending.

As with all events involving the labyrinth, care must be taken to ensure that the workshop selected is appropriate for both the space and the people attending. A small space that only just fits in a labyrinth, for example, will not be an easy place in which to hold a 'Creative Responses' workshop. Equally, a large, potentially noisy space, open to the public, might not be conducive to a workshop that requires much personal input and reflection. It is essential to liaise closely with the originators of the event to determine exactly what facilities are available and how any potential difficulties might be overcome.

Practicalities must not be ignored – if you are planning an all-day workshop, what sort of facilities will be

available at the location, for example? It is always useful if someone from the organization can be around to
help with practical matters, and this is the best option
if it is possible. If not, you will need to know where the
toilets are, and whether there are facilities for making tea
and coffee. Without being over-anxious, it is worthwhile
checking whether you will be expected to bring your own
supplies of coffee, tea, milk, biscuits etc. – some places
will not have these available to the general public. If you
do need to bring your own provisions, try to make them
as appealing as possible – labyrinth experiences can be
emotionally draining, and good-quality hospitality will
help participants feel cared for.

Find out what facilities are available for meals – whether
participants are expected to leave the workshop space for
these or to bring their own food. If you are using a portable labyrinth, will this need to be put away at this time,
or is there space around it for eating and socializing?

If the labyrinth is an outdoor one, establish what the
fall-back arrangements are if the weather is inclement.
You may have a canvas labyrinth you can bring for an
indoor walk, or there may be space for you to mark one
out with masking tape (see the Appendix).

Workshop timetable

This must be developed with the organizers of the
event, allowing particular sections of the workshop to
be expanded if circumstances require it – for example,
a seasoned labyrinth walking group may need only a
brief introductory talk, although it is always wise to put
your particular workshop in your own context in order

to avoid misunderstandings. For this reason too, I have found it sensible to begin and end a workshop with an act of worship, to remind participants that the labyrinth walk is not an end in itself, but merely a tool to enable a deeper relationship with God.

In order to exploit fully all that the labyrinth has to offer as a path of prayer, a full-day workshop is the best option, but much that is good and useful can be obtained from a half-day workshop, although care must be taken to avoid a feeling of being rushed or that one's time on the labyrinth is uncomfortably limited.

Possible timetable for a labyrinth workshop

10.00–10.15 a.m. – Gathering and opening worship
10.15–10.30 a.m. – Talk 1
10.30–10.45 a.m. – Break for coffee
10.45 a.m.–12.00 p.m. – Labyrinth walk
12.00–12.15 p.m. – Talk 2
12.15–1.30 p.m. – Labyrinth walk
1.30–2.00 p.m. – Break for lunch
2.00–2.15 p.m. – Talk 3
2.15–3.30 p.m. – Labyrinth walk
3.30–4.00 p.m. – Plenary session and closing worship

Workshop worship
MORNING WORSHIP

GATHERING

The day's journey has begun
Let us walk together with God in his ways.
Direct our footsteps, Lord
Along your paths.

Gracious God, help us to be mindful of your presence
  today.
Guide us through its events and encounters,
Bless our words and our actions,
Help us to see your face in the face of those we meet and
Give us the grace to begin, engage with
And end this day in your love and truthfulness. **Amen**

CONFESSION

Good and upright is the Lord; therefore he instructs
sinners in his ways. We remember those times when we
have strayed from God's ways. For the sake of your name,
Lord, forgive our iniquity, though it is great.

Silence

**Father of all, we come before you humble in heart, seeking
your pardon for those times when we have not walked in
your way or followed your directions. We know that in
you is the path of life; help us to journey on in your light,
putting the darkness of our misdeeds and words behind
us.**

ABSOLUTION

All the ways of the Lord are loving and faithful towards
those who keep the demands of his covenant. Let us walk
on forgiven and rejoicing.

OLD TESTAMENT READING

You have searched me, LORD,
and you know me.
You know when I sit and when I rise;
you perceive my thoughts from afar.
You discern my going out and my lying down;
you are familiar with all my ways.
Before a word is on my tongue
you, LORD, know it completely.
You hem me in behind and before,
and you lay your hand upon me.
Such knowledge is too wonderful for me,
too lofty for me to attain.

Where can I go from your Spirit?
Where can I flee from your presence?
If I go up to the heavens, you are there;
if I make my bed in the depths, you are there.
If I rise on the wings of the dawn,
if I settle on the far side of the sea,
even there your hand will guide me,
your right hand will hold me fast.
If I say, 'Surely the darkness will hide me
and the light become night around me,'
even the darkness will not be dark to you;

the night will shine like the day,
for darkness is as light to you.
Psalm 139.1–12 (NIV)

NEW TESTAMENT READING

'Do not let your hearts be troubled. You believe in God;
believe also in me. My Father's house has many rooms;
if that were not so, would I have told you that I am
going there to prepare a place for you? And if I go and
prepare a place for you, I will come back and take you
to be with me that you also may be where I am. You
know the way to the place where I am going.' Thomas
said to him, 'Lord, we don't know where you are going,
so how can we know the way?' Jesus answered, 'I am
the way and the truth and the life. No one comes to the
Father except through me.
John 14.1–6 (NIV)

Silence

PRAYERS

The Almighty and everlasting God, Who is the Way,
the Truth, and the Life, dispose your journey according
to His good pleasure; send his angel Raphael to keep
you in this your pilgrimage, and both conduct you in
peace on your way to the place where you would be,
and bring you back again on your return to us in safety.
Sarum Missal 1150

Almighty God, whose only Son has opened for us a
new and living way into your presence: give us pure
hearts and steadfast wills to worship you in spirit and
in truth; through Jesus Christ your Son our Lord, who
is alive and reigns with you, in the unity of the Holy
Spirit, one God, now and for ever.
Collect for Trinity 14
(*from* Common Worship, *page 416*)

GRACE

**The grace of our Lord Jesus Christ, the love of God
and the fellowship of the Holy Spirit be with us all,
evermore, Amen**

Lord, guide us on our journeys as we leave this place
**You will show us the path of life, fullness of joy is in
your presence, Amen**

Workshop worship
EVENING WORSHIP

GATHERING

We gather at the end of the day
Meeting together to rest in your peace.
As the sun sets on our labours, Lord
So may the light of your love guide us through the night.

We give thanks for a day now ending,
For its joys and discoveries,
Its learning and encounters.
Guide us and guard us as we journey on
And keep us always mindful of the constancy of your
     presence. **Amen**

CONFESSION

We confess the times that our ways have been crooked,
the occasions when we have strayed from the path of
righteousness.

Silence

ABSOLUTION

You are precious and God loves you. Continue on your
journey as forgiven people. Let the word of God be a
lamp to your feet and a light to your path.

OLD TESTAMENT READING

The Eternal is my shepherd, He cares for me always.
He provides me rest in rich, green fields
beside streams of refreshing water.
He soothes my fears;
He makes me whole again,
steering me off worn, hard paths
to roads where truth and righteousness echo His
    name.

Even in the unending shadows of death's darkness,
I am not overcome by fear.
Because You are with me in those dark moments,
near with Your protection and guidance,
I am comforted.

You spread out a table before me,
provisions in the midst of attack from my enemies;
You care for all my needs,
anointing my head with soothing, fragrant oil,
filling my cup again and again with Your grace.
Certainly Your faithful protection and loving
    provision will pursue me where I go, always,
    everywhere.
I will always be with the Eternal, in Your house forever.
Psalm 23 (The Voice)

NEW TESTAMENT READING

I am the good shepherd. The good shepherd lays down
His life for the sheep in His care. The hired hand is
not like the shepherd caring for His own sheep. When
a wolf attacks, snatching and scattering the sheep, he

runs for his life, leaving them defenseless. The hired hand runs because he works only for wages and does not care for the sheep. I am the good shepherd; I know My sheep, and My sheep know Me. As the Father knows Me, I know the Father; I will give My life for the sheep.
John 10.11–15 (The Voice)

Silence

PRAYERS

Merciful Father, you gave your Son Jesus Christ to be the good shepherd, and in his love for us to lay down his life and rise again: keep us always under his protection, and give us grace to follow in his steps; through Jesus Christ our Lord.
Post Communion for Easter 4
(*from* Common Worship, *page 402*)

God of our pilgrimage, you have led us to the living water: refresh and sustain us as we go forward on our journey, in the name of Jesus Christ our Lord.
Post Communion for Trinity 6
(*from* Common Worship, *page 411*)

GRACE

The grace of our Lord Jesus Christ, the love of God and the fellowship of the Holy Spirit be with us all, evermore, Amen

Lord, guide us on our journeys as we leave this place
You will show us the path of life.

Suggestions for an introductory talk on labyrinths

This can be made as long or short as you have time for. If there are facilities for showing slides, pictures can be a very useful way of highlighting the differences between mazes and labyrinths and also for illustrating the characteristics of different styles of labyrinths.

Include some information on the layout of the day, and your expectations of how it will unfold. Reassure participants that all sessions are completely voluntary and that if anyone feels uncomfortable with anything that happens they are free to stop. Remind participants that events within the workshop should be seen as confidential and confined to those attending the workshop.

You might want to share how you first became involved with labyrinths and other information about your spiritual background. Do not go into too much detail – the workshop is not about you, but designed to enable and resource the participants!

It is important to begin with a definition of a labyrinth so that there is no confusion from the start. In the simplest terms, a labyrinth is a single pathway, turning and twisting upon itself in a complex pattern into a single central point. From the entrance to the labyrinth, if the path is followed faithfully, the centre will always be arrived at. If the same path, the only path, is taken, the walker will return to the entrance. Differentiate this from a maze, which offers a number of pathways, some of which will lead nowhere. A labyrinth is designed to enable, not confuse. It is possible to lose oneself in a maze – labyrinths are for finding both self and God.

You might want to introduce some element of discussion as to the relationship of the labyrinth with other faiths – as a symbol of pilgrimage, for example. It is advisable to continue to reinforce the Christian context within which you will be working, and to offer some of the different ways in which a labyrinth can be used:

- Providing a starting point for exploring the nature of one's spirituality.
- Acting as an aid to prayer and a method of meditation.
- Enabling us to engage in or deepen our relationship with God.

Material from Chapter 1 of this book can be incorporated into this section to give a brief outline of the history of labyrinths up to the present time.

Describe the nature and pattern of the labyrinth being used for the workshop – if it is Chartres style, you might want to describe the Chartres labyrinth itself and how it differs from the one in use.

Reassure participants that anything they do on the labyrinth is valid – it is a spiritual tool, not a trap. All that is necessary is to follow the path to the centre and then out again, and not even that if it feels wrong! If the workshop has a particular theme, encourage participants to engage with the thoughts and reflections you have offered. If it is simply an open walk, then attentive expectation is all that is needed.

Don't forget to introduce some simple etiquette for walkers: in order to feel comfortable on the labyrinth, a gap should be left between walkers. Decide how large a gap this should be according to the size of the labyrinth, the number of workshop participants, and the time available. To allow for variations of pace, it is best to allocate a point on the labyrinth as the place where the walker in front should have arrived before the next walker enters. As there is only one path, walkers will meet each other on the way in and out. Stepping aside courteously is all that is necessary – there is no need for acknowledgement if it is not felt to be appropriate. Walkers should not feel inhibited by the pace of the walker in front – overtaking is acceptable, as is being overtaken; the labyrinth is a reflection space, not a race track. Witnessing others walking the labyrinth is as much part of the experience as actually walking it – remind the participants to remain silent after they have completed their walk and to hold the space respectfully for the rest of the group.

Reassure participants that they do not have to continue to walk if they feel physically or spiritually uncomfortable. The labyrinth can be emotionally disturbing as walkers are brought face to face with inmost thoughts and feelings. It can also be a physical challenge, particularly for those with balance issues or muscular limitations. Similarly they are not to be concerned if they lose the path or end up in the centre once more when they were expecting to arrive at the outside. Whichever direction one walks in, either the centre or the outside will eventually be arrived at and all that is then necessary is to turn around and follow the path back in or out.

Encourage participants to use everything that happens to them on the labyrinth as material for reflection – as a metaphor of their lives. Remind them to remain open to their experience and to keep listening for what God might want to say to them.

Workshop outline 1: The labyrinth – a history

Introduction

This is a very basic workshop and can be used for introducing the idea of labyrinth to people who are new to its spirituality. It offers a brief history of labyrinth and gives it a spiritual context. It is an expanded version of the brief introduction given on p. 24, so this element of the workshop does not need to be included. The main themes to this workshop are the idea of the Sinai Desert as a symbolic labyrinth, and how we can use desert times within our own lives, and the labyrinth as a symbol of our own spiritual journey, and the insights we might gain from that. Finally, the tension between the freedom of the labyrinth within a confined space is explored with reference to our freedom in Christ, the Way, the Truth and the Life.

Because much of the reflection requires walking the labyrinth itself, this timetable is only suitable for a smaller labyrinth – a 24'/7.3m Chartres one, for example. The full 42'/12.8m labyrinths might necessitate a longer workshop time, or even for the event to be spread over two days.

Talk 1

The labyrinth is an archetypal pattern – it appears both in nature and in the patterns and drawings made by many civilizations through the centuries. Natural phenomena such as the whorls on seashells and fingerprints, the movements of winds and tides, the convolutions of the brain itself, all echo the twisting and turnings of the single labyrinth path. Labyrinth patterns exist in Mayan, Roman, Egyptian, Chinese and European civilizations, often related to religious or spiritual purposes, and from as early as the fourth century AD such patterns began to appear in churches. These at first were small but, as building techniques improved, these finger labyrinths became large designs, often filling the floor of the nave in which they were installed. However, although many labyrinths were constructed in the medieval period, they fell out of use and at the end of the eighteenth century were destroyed, only coming into mainstream Christian use in the later part of the twentieth century with the revival of interest in this meditative pathway as a way of deepening a relationship with God.

Opponents to the use of the labyrinth for Christian purposes cite not only its use by pagans and new age spiritualities but the absence of the labyrinth from the Bible. To the first argument, one can state that many Christian traditions, particularly our festivals, were in fact adapted from pagan use and 'sanctified' thereby in a way that should not prevent us from making use of a spiritual tool that, like pilgrimage, is found in many religious contexts.

It is true that the labyrinth is not mentioned in the Bible, and it has been argued that this is because previous civilizations made use of the labyrinth to symbolize some aspect of death – labyrinth patterns were traced on doors to trap the spirits of the dead; for the Mayan Indians, the labyrinth was the pathway travelled after death; and the Roman writer Virgil tells of a labyrinth set into the gates of hell. For the Jewish people, the symbolizing of a journey after death was not needed – the dead waited in the liminal Sheol for resurrection at a future date. However, the metaphor of the labyrinth, it could be argued, under-pins both the Old and the New Testaments.

The spiritual geography of the Old Testament has at its heart a huge desert – the Sinai – out of which a trembling terrified group of refugees emerged as a nation with an identity and a purpose. Physically the desert would not have taken 40 years to cross, but for a people to emerge as the children of God, it was necessary that none of the generation that entered the desert should leave it, but instead pass on the task to those renewed by their time in the wilderness. The desert thus becomes a symbol of a time of testing and trial, but one from which something new and extraordinary emerges.

The endless crossings and re-crossings of a single piece of land are reflected in the pattern of the labyrinth. Within the pattern, new insights are gained and know-ledge found, to enable walkers better to engage with the world beyond the labyrinth.

It is a good idea to include here some guidelines on walking a labyrinth, its etiquette and the importance of witnessing the walk of others. As usual, stress that the reflections pro-vided are only suggestions and that each walker is free to use the labyrinth in the way they feel is best.

Reflection 1

You will need enough small pots of dry soil so that every-one can have one, a jug of water and some seeds. Place the water and seeds in the centre of the labyrinth.

Take a pot of soil and, as you stand at the entrance to the labyrinth, look at it carefully. See how dry it is – it cannot sustain life as it lacks the vital ingredient of water. As you walk into the labyrinth, holding the pot, think about the dry times of your life – those times when your prayer life seemed unsatisfactory, or your relationship with God was not as deep or sustaining as you would like. Hold these times in your heart and ask God to send you refreshment. When you get to the centre, water the pot and plant a seed. Jesus said 'I am the living water; whoever comes to me will never be thirsty.' Look at the pot that now contains the promise of new life and growth. Pray that the seeds of new life in your heart will flourish and grow, watered by prayer and sustained by grace. Take the pot out of the labyrinth and carry it on with you.

Talk 2

Jesus does not use a labyrinth, that is undeniable; however, a similar pattern is evident if we look at the journeyings of Christ's life. Jesus did not stay for long in one place during the time of his ministry, but neither did he travel to far-off, distant lands. The places he visited, those blessed by his presence or where healings took place, are all in one tiny area of a small part of the world, and Christ wove his way back and forth throughout this area, creating a beautiful fabric with the threads of his travelling, decorated with healings and parables, love and compassion. This extraordinary ministry was only possible because he frequently took time away from the crowd, and even from his disciples, to reflect and pray, to deepen his relationship with God and to gain strength for future events. The last journey of Christ also winds its way steadily to that central point on a hilltop, where the heart of things is achieved and redeemed.

Our wanderings on the labyrinth echo Christ's journey, and provide us with space for reflection and prayer so that we too can enter into the heart of things, and return to the outside world equipped with all that is necessary.

Reflection 2

You will need a pile of stones – there should be enough for everyone to have at least five.

Jesus often took time away from people and situations that demanded much of him, in order to reflect and pray. As you stand outside the labyrinth, think of those situations and people that obscure your relationship with God. They may be people who demand a lot of you, difficult situations, or circumstances that preoccupy you. Think also of other things that may obstruct your path – a yearning for material possessions, too much focus on work, an addiction to a substance. For each obstruction, pick up a stone. Take these stones with you as you journey into the labyrinth – notice what a nuisance they are, how they make your journey more cumbersome and difficult. When you reach the centre, ask God for the grace to lay all your preoccupations and obstructions at his feet, so that he might remove them from your path. Walk freely out of the labyrinth, rejoicing.

Talk 3

One good reason for using a Chartres-style labyrinth, or at least one that has a Chartres-style pattern, is that its ecclesiastical credentials are impeccable! Sometime between 1194 and 1220, the labyrinth was laid into the floor of the nave of the cathedral in Chartres, in blocks of dark blue and white stone. The 42'/12.8m-wide design, with its path of 861½'/263m in total, made a significant impact on the visitor as they entered the building, drawing the eye forward and upward to the great east window with the high altar below. Too elaborate to be merely a maker's mark, the labyrinth's design fits in perfectly with the rest of the structure of the cathedral, providing balance and harmony, enhancing the sacred geometry of the structure with its dependence on the 12-pointed star, and its mathematical relationship with the rest of the building. And Chartres was not the only cathedral to install such a design – this was echoed throughout France and in parts of Germany, Italy and England as well. Although most of these labyrinths were later demolished, using such a tool for meditation and prayer does not herald a return to pagan times, but rather uses the gifts that have been given to us by past Christians to enhance our own prayer life today. Nowadays, research is beginning to show the mental and physical benefits of walking the labyrinth – the spiritual ones have been acknowledged for centuries.

Reflection 3

For this final walk, try to have a completely open mind. Do not enter with a specific purpose, only a willingness to listen and a sensitivity to the voice of God. As you walk, allow your mind to range freely. Any distracting thoughts that enter your head can be noted, and given up to God. Pause in the centre, and ask God to speak to you.

Workshop outline 2: Pilgrimage

This workshop combines both the historical and the spiritual. It gives a brief outline of the nature of pilgrimage and its uses within Christian spirituality and also offers, through a symbolic pilgrimage on the labyrinth, a way of encouraging participants to think about their own spiritual journey. In the suggested timetable below, the labyrinth walk takes place at the end of the workshop, with shorter periods for reflection throughout the day. If the labyrinth is a small one, participants can be invited to walk the labyrinth during these reflection times. If this is the case, then the introduction to the labyrinth needs, obviously, to be at the beginning of the day. Alternatively, finger labyrinths or labyrinth beads can be provided (see Appendix for instructions).

Possible timetable for pilgrimage workshop

10.00–10.20 a.m. – Gathering and opening worship
10.20–10.30 a.m. – Talk 1
10.30–10.50 a.m. – Reflection
10.50–11.00 a.m. – Talk 2
11.00–11.20 a.m. – Reflection
11.20–11.40 a.m. – Break for coffee
11.40–11.50 a.m. – Talk 3
11.50 a.m.–12.10 p.m. – Reflection
12.10–12.20 p.m. – Talk 4
12.20–12.40 p.m. – Reflection
12.40–1.30 p.m. – Lunch
1.30–1.45 p.m. – Brief introduction to walking the labyrinth

1.45–3.00 p.m. – Walking the labyrinth
3.00–3.30 p.m. – Plenary session
3.30–4.00 p.m. – Closing worship and tea

Talk 1: 'Take nothing for the journey'

> When Jesus had called the Twelve together, he gave them power and authority to drive out all demons and to cure diseases, and he sent them out to proclaim the kingdom of God and to heal those who were ill. He told them: 'Take nothing for the journey – no staff, no bag, no bread, no money, no extra shirt.'
> *Luke 9.1–3* (NIV)

Pilgrimage is a spiritual journey to a sacred place. From earliest times, people have been drawn to certain places where it was felt that the gap between heaven and earth was slightly less – 'thin' places. Journeys were also made to the sites of famous events, such as those of the life of Christ, and the graves of saints. Originally it was believed that a journey to these places offered the traveller an improved chance of success for their prayers, but many other motives have impelled pilgrims throughout the years. Some travel because they wish to offer a penance for their crime; others to ask for physical or spiritual healing. Many sought an opportunity to escape the humdrum nature of their everyday lives, but many more sought, and still seek, time to reflect on their life so far, space to listen to God, and an opportunity to decide how best to move forward in their remaining years on earth.

In medieval times, preparation for such a long and dangerous journey as a pilgrimage to Santiago de Compostela, Rome or even Jerusalem was a lengthy business.

Permission had to be gained, wills drawn up, debts cleared, and the regulation pilgrim's clothing of cloak, hat, staff and bag had to be obtained, along with the all-important *testimonials* that certified the validity of the pilgrim's journey and offered accommodation and a certain degree of protection from harassment along the way. Today, along with the usual complexities of travel arrangements, similar difficult decisions must be made about which items of clothing or equipment should be included in a pack that will always weigh more than its owner wants it to!

However, more important than the physical items that are taken on the journey, and far more crucial to the success of the expedition, is the mental attitude. The pilgrim must abandon narrowness of heart and mind and a pre-judging disposition and take instead an openness to all experiences and a readiness to embrace all events that occur upon the way.

Reflection 1

You will need a pile of small stones. There should be enough for every participant to have at least five. Invite participants to gather a handful of stones before beginning this exercise.

Reflect on the attitudes and prejudices that you carry with you on your journey through life. Some of these are unnecessary and difficult to travel with – a materialist anxiety about the future, a tendency towards suspicion of the motives of others, a resentment of the hindrances that have been placed in your path.

Determine to take with you only the important things – your beliefs, your love for those with whom you share your life, a generous spirit and an open heart.

Consider your journey of life from this point onwards, and reflect on the luggage that you are taking with you on this journey. Using your handful of stones, make a small pile of those items that must be taken with you – a dependent relative or friend, an illness or disability, a close relationship. Place them by your seat, or where you have been standing. Try to make this pile of stones as small as possible. When you have finished it, thank God for the people and circumstances that are contained within it. Ask him for his help in carrying your burdens when they seem too heavy for you to bear, and for the grace that you may use them for the glory of his kingdom. If you wish, you can carry this pile of stones with you into the centre of the labyrinth during your walk, praying over them as you do so, and offering them to God in the centre. You can leave them there or return with them to your seat after your walk.

Now take some more stones and use them to build a pile of those people and attitudes that no longer need to accompany you on your journey – guilt over a failed relationship, the wounding criticisms of others, attitudes of pride or envy that poison your response to your circumstances, a dependence on particular comforts such as food or drink. When the pile is finished, ask God for his help in leaving these unnecessary burdens behind, and for the grace to travel on more lightly, open to the events that the journey may bring. If you wish, you can leave these stones at the entrance to the labyrinth at the start of your walk.

Talk 2: 'Do not worry about tomorrow'

> So do not worry, saying 'What shall we eat?' or 'What shall we drink?' or 'What shall we wear?' For the pagans run after all these things, and your heavenly Father knows that you need them. But seek first his kingdom and his righteousness and all these things shall be given to you as well. Therefore do not worry about tomorrow, for tomorrow will worry about itself. Each day has enough trouble of its own.
>
> *Matthew 6.31–34* (NIV)

For medieval pilgrims, going on a long journey to a distant place was a huge undertaking. Although the landscape and places near the pilgrim's home would be extremely familiar, it would not be long before the traveller would be forced to rely on others for information about the route ahead, and would have to take great care to follow the correct path rather than one that might lead them astray. These routes might be blocked by floods or fallen trees, they might lead through towns suffering from the plague, or through lonely forests which were the haunt of bandits. Always, the pilgrim would be aware of the landscape he was journeying through, often less sensitive to its beauties than its dangers.

For most people today, our relationship with the landscape is not so intense. Motorized travel, maps and satnav have all combined to make a proposed journey into a simple logistical task. There is little of the danger, but little of the adventure as well. For the pilgrim on foot, the relationship with the landscape is once more renewed as streams are negotiated, hills climbed, and the rich variety of nature encountered in an intensity that we have all but lost today.

Reflection 2

If the weather and location permit, invite participants to go outside and gather five bits of vegetation, in various stages of growth and deterioration. Try to have at least five, from seeds and young shoots, to plants in full leaf, and old, dying or dead leaves and plants. If this is not possible for any reason, provide a pile of leaves, flowers or foliage for the participants to choose from. If this workshop takes place during winter months, seeds can be obtained from packets, and you may find it necessary to buy the younger plants from garden centres. From the middle of winter, small pots of indoor seedlings are usually available.

The weather is changing and unceasingly variable. These changes are an integral part of the survival of the landscape – rain and wind are needed as much as sun and heat if the natural world is to grow and flourish. Indeed, too much or too little of any sort of weather brings disaster – draught or floods, crop failure and destruction. So too are the times and seasons of our lives, each changing, each important in its own way. Take the five pieces of vegetation that you have gathered, and place these in front of you, carefully separating them out. Look at them closely, and notice the uniqueness of each, even though they are in themselves insignificant. Then think to yourself how all God's love went into creating those plants ... that God loves them, that they are irreplaceable, that they are special to God. Marvel at the miracle that created them. Then remind yourself that God loves you, that all his love for all creation was poured out in creating you, redeeming you for his own.

Now consider where in your life you are – are you a young shoot or are you already showing signs of age and decay? Think of the joys associated with each season of your life and allow yourself to anticipate the joys of the season to come. Now reflect on your spiritual life – are you in the same place as your physical life or are you as yet unfruitful, still a seed? Or perhaps you feel your spiritual life to be dead and needing to be revived. Ask God to help you blossom spiritually in whatever time of life you have reached. Thank him for the joys of your life and also for the sorrows – in themselves as important to growth and flourishing as times of gladness. Gather your bouquet together and leave it where you will be able to see it throughout the day, and give thanks whenever you do.

To see a World in a Grain of Sand
And a Heaven in a Wild Flower
Hold Infinity in the palm of your hand
And Eternity in an hour ...
William Blake, 1757–1827
(*from 'Auguries of Innocence'*)

Talk 3: 'How can we know the way?'

'Do not let your hearts be troubled. You believe in God; believe also in me. My Father's house has many rooms; if that were not so, would I have told you that I am going there to prepare a place for you? And if I go and prepare a place for you, I will come back and take you to be with me that you also may be where I am. You know the way to the place where I am going.' Thomas

said to him, 'Lord, we don't know where you are going, so how can we know the way?' Jesus answered: 'I am the way and the truth and the life. No one comes to the Father except through me.'
John 14.1–6 (NIV)

As well as major events to overcome, such as shipwrecks, attacks from brigands and encounters with the plague, earlier pilgrims had many minor things to worry about as well. The variability of food and a long distance between fresh water supplies could both threaten the health of the pilgrim. One's fellow travellers could also be a threat – tales are recorded of thieves joining pilgrim parties in order to strip them of their money and possessions, often abandoning them in a foreign country with no means of completing their journey. It would have been easy to spend the entire pilgrimage in an advanced state of anxiety and stress.

Even today, pilgrims have their concerns. Fresh water is not always easy to find, and accommodation, especially for the more popular routes, can be overbooked, leading to much anxiety about where to stay the night. However, constant worrying about the possibility of the next disaster will take away much of the pleasure of the journey – better to save one's strength in order to deal more successfully with the situation if it arises than waste energy in anticipation!

Reflection 3

You will need a pile of largish stones, about the size of a child's fist. These can be obtained in bags from a garden centre, or collected from outside.

Find a stone that appeals to you – either in its size and shape, or its colour. Pick it up and examine it carefully. Notice each detail of the stone's appearance – its sharp edges and rough corners. The stone has been shaped this way over hundreds of years by the actions of its surroundings – it has rubbed against other stones, been soaked by rain, and frozen by cold. All these have made the stone the way it is today, and its appeal is not necessarily in its beauty but in the variety of its shape and texture. Consider your own heart, how that has been shaped by the actions of others and yourself. Some of those actions, both good and bad, have made you stronger, others have left you damaged and weak, but all of them have made you the unique person you are, capable of fulfilling the particular purpose God has in mind for you. Give thanks for your life so far, and place the stone, now warmed by your hands, carefully back into the landscape.

Workshop outline 3: Celebrating seasons – change and growth in different stages of life

Introduction

The potential danger of a workshop that celebrates the different times and seasons in life is that it often tends to focus on older people and can be somewhat gloomy in outlook. This workshop is designed for people of all ages and in all stages of life as an aid to reflection on the changes that are a part of all human life. The workshop looks at seasons not as directly relating to one particular age or stage in life – spring being equated with youth, for example, and old age with winter is neither helpful nor productive. Rather, it looks at life as a whole and the constant growth and decay that occurs in all our lives – while some parts of our lives are flourishing, others might not be doing so well. Equally, there is a time for certain activities, and another time when either those activities are no longer possible or there is not yet the space and energy for them. This workshop helps us to examine every part of our lives and look both to the past and to the future to gain an understanding of the present.

Talk 1: Summer/autumn – time to rejoice

For everything there is a season, and a time for every matter under heaven: a time to be born, and a time to die; a time to plant, and a time to pluck up what is planted; a time to kill, and a time to heal; a time to break down, and a time to build up; a time to weep, and a time to laugh; a time to mourn, and a time to dance; a

time to throw away stones, and a time to gather stones together; a time to embrace, and a time to refrain from embracing; a time to seek, and a time to lose; a time to keep, and a time to throw away; a time to tear, and a time to sew; a time to keep silence, and a time to speak; a time to love, and a time to hate; a time for war, and a time for peace.
Ecclesiastes 3.1–8 (NRSV)

This reading is a very popular one at funerals and memorial services and for good reason – it reassures us that the things that happen to us are not without reason, that they are part of our human condition, and that there are as many good, healing events as there are difficult and challenging occasions. However, the danger can be that it is read as a chronological record: that a time to lose follows on from a time of seeking, a time of sewing is the consequence of a time of tearing. Life, as we know, is more complicated than that and, at any one time, good constructive events can be happening alongside painful and damaging occurrences. During the workshop, participants will be encouraged to examine different aspects of their lives and try to discern in what stage of growth or decay some of these aspects may be found.

Awe came upon everyone, because many wonders and signs were being done by the apostles. All who believed were together and had all things in common; they would sell their possessions and goods and distribute the proceeds to all, as any had need. Day by day, as they spent much time together in the temple, they broke bread at home and ate their food with glad and generous hearts, praising God and having the goodwill of all the people.

And day by day the Lord added to their number those
who were being saved.
Acts 2.43–47 (NRSV)

This is a wonderful picture of an ideal community, and
one that we all might aspire to. It is a picture of a group
of people who have got their priorities right – possessions
and material goods no longer have the psychological
stranglehold that they do on so many of us. All things are
shared equally for the common good and there is no fear-
ful holding back or greedy acquisitiveness. Community
is valued above all else, and those who are less fortunate
are helped by others in the group. The main focus of the
people is worship and praise for the God who created
them and the result is a harmonious and joyful way of
existence.

All too often it is easy to look at our lives and high-
light that which is difficult or unsatisfactory about them
– relationships can be testing, work or the lack of it can
dominate our thinking, and we can easily become pre-
occupied with the getting and keeping of all manner of
material things, many times deluding ourselves that this
is for a higher purpose such as the future wellbeing of the
family or security against possible disaster. At such times
it is easy to feel bereft of the joy that those early disciples
experienced in the company of each other and of God.
But for most of us, however challenging times may seem,
there will be something to rejoice about. Perhaps there
is some achievement that has finally been attained, some
skill that is being honed to our satisfaction, some part of
our lives that brings us joy or comfort, whether it is the
company of a good friend, the pleasure to be found in
a place of our own, the enjoyment of a pastime, or the

spiritual refreshment from a church service or event. We are reminded in the Holy Communion Service that not only is it right to give thanks and praise to God, it is 'our duty and our joy at all times and in all places' to do so.

Reflection 1

You will need green pipe cleaners (about a dozen per person), scissors, coloured tissue paper.

Spend some time reflecting on all the things that bring you joy in your life. They might be significant events or major things – such as a happy partnership, a friend, a child – or small things such as reading a good book or taking a long walk. For each thing that causes you to give thanks, cut circles of the tissue paper and make a flower out of them, by scrunching them together at one end and binding them with a pipe cleaner stem. You can make them large or small, or keep them all the same size.

Talk 2: Winter – time to leave behind

> I am the true vine and my Father is the gardener. He cuts off every branch in me that bears no fruit, while every branch that does bear fruit he prunes so that it will be even more fruitful.
> *John 15.1–2* (NIV)

Near the end of the year, just when autumn is creeping imperceptibly towards winter, the harvest is over and the sap has sunk back from the leaves, causing them to fade and fall, it is pruning time. The careful gardener takes a pair of secateurs and spends many hours clipping away at the stems and branches of shrubs and trees in the garden. Old, dying wood is cut back ruthlessly, sometimes nearly as far as the trunk itself. Other branches may also be cut off – those that are growing contrariwise, at odds with the overall shape of the tree or shrub, those that rub against other branches or impede their growth. Sometimes bolder measures are called for and the pruning saw is used to remove significant pieces of wood whose attachment to the tree draws vital energy away from those areas that need it most. Finally the work is done, and the plants are ready for winter. Their shape is cleaner and clearer, revealing the distinctiveness of each variety of tree and shrub. Space has been made for the new growth that will arrive in the spring, that same growth that even now the garden is preparing for, silently, below the quiet, seemingly dead surface of a winter garden.

Removing from our lives those habits and affections that cause us harm is very often painful. Although we may be aware that certain activities and behaviours damage not only ourselves but the people and environment around us, it can still be a heart-wrenchingly difficult activity to identify them and then abstain from them. Perhaps these actions were once necessary and even useful, just as the branches of a tree were once alive and flourishing, but now are dead and serve no purpose. Perhaps they are simply habits formed at a time when such things were desirable and effective but now have lost meaning and purpose, although we might still cling to them for comfort and as a reminder of other times. None the less, if we are to thrive and to fulfil truly our potential as God's children, we must learn to identify damaging and dangerous ways of speaking and acting and destroy them.

This identification process can be challenging and hurtful, and the removal process even more so. However, it is necessary to cut away the dead wood of non-productive and harmful thoughts and actions in order that our true selves can flourish. It is only then that we can use our precious energy and attention for the purpose for which it was created.

Reflection 2

You will need bare twigs or small branches.

Reflect on those activities and habits of speech and action that are harmful and dangerous to you or to others. Each time you have identified one, select a twig or branch and place it among the bunch of tissue flowers that you have created. As you add more and more to the bunch, notice how they affect the shape and pattern of the flowers, providing areas of starkness in among the bright colours of the tissue. Reflect on the effects of your own actions on all that you love and cherish.

When your bouquet is complete, you might want to carry it into the labyrinth. At the centre, remove the dead sticks from among the flowers and place them in the bowl provided. If it is possible, a fire can be kindled from these sticks, as those destructive habits and affections are themselves destroyed. Walk out of the labyrinth bringing your flowers with you.

Talk 3: Spring – time to nurture

> He put before them another parable: 'The kingdom of
> heaven is like a mustard seed that someone took and
> sowed in his field; it is the smallest of all the seeds,
> but when it has grown it is the greatest of shrubs and
> becomes a tree, so that the birds of the air come and
> make nests in its branches.'
> *Matthew 13.31–32* (NRSV)

We hear this parable many times in our lives – so many
in fact that we may be in danger of hearing it without
listening to it as attentively as we might. It is a bit of a
truism in secular life as well – 'mighty oaks from little
acorns grow' shares the same wisdom with us; all that it
takes is one small seed, one step, one germ of an idea, to
make something wonderful happen. And those seeds are
within all of us. It may seem as if we are stuck in winter at
the moment, that everything in our lives is bleak and non-
productive. We may feel triumphantly flourishing, but at
the same time anxious about whether this flourishing can
be sustained. But throughout the darkest winter, the seeds
of the future are hidden in the soil, simply waiting for
the right time to begin to grow; and even in the height of
summer, seeds are being developed, ready for dropping
in the autumn so that the cycle can begin again. Mother
Teresa, the nun who did so much to help the poor and
dying in Calcutta, started her mission with just 30 pence,
but as she said to those who tried to dissuade her, she
had 30 pence and God, which meant she was unbeatable.
There is a story that a man approached Mother Teresa
one day and said, 'Mother, I want to do something great
for God, but I don't know what. Should I start a school,

be a missionary in a foreign land, build up a charitable agency?' He had great visions. Mother Teresa looked at him closely, with kindness, and responded: 'What you need to do is make sure that no one in your family goes unloved.' So sometimes even the smallest gestures, the smallest beginnings, can be enough to show someone the love of God, or to start something wonderful that will help to usher in the kingdom.

Reflection 3

You will need a variety of seeds of different sizes, from small poppy seeds to something large like pumpkin or sunflower seeds. Allow a generous handful in a small pot for each participant.

Look at the seeds in your pot – all different sizes and shapes. Were you to look under a microscope you would see something even more amazing, for all these seeds are the most wonderfully complex and colourful objects. Just as God pours all his love and creativity into these tiny seeds, some of which will produce flowers that only blossom for a few days or weeks, so he has created each one of us with enormous love for the potential he sees within us. As you walk the labyrinth, hold the pot of seeds carefully before you, reflecting on the new beginnings in your life – new relationships, new events. Some of these may be very tentative, some perhaps difficult to undertake but, as you reflect on them, try to discern whether they will produce good fruit that will benefit both you and others, and whether as such they are enterprises that are worth continuing with.

Workshop outline 4: Calling and vocation

Introduction

This workshop can be used in a number of ways. It can be used as part of a Diocesan Day exploring vocations to ordained ministry, or as a tool for reflection by those already on the path of discernment towards a selection conference. However, it can also be used as part of a parish initiative to enable members of a parish or congregation to reflect on the gifts that they could offer the church and the wider community, and how best to live out their calling as Christians within their own circumstances.

Talk 1

> As he walked by the Sea of Galilee, he saw two brothers, Simon, who is called Peter, and Andrew his brother, casting a net into the lake – for they were fishermen. And he said to them, 'Follow me, and I will make you fish for people.' Immediately they left their nets and followed him. As he went from there, he saw two other brothers, James son of Zebedee and his brother John, in the boat with their father Zebedee, mending their nets, and he called them. Immediately they left the boat and their father, and followed him.
> *Matthew 4.18–22* (NRSV)

The first call of Christ is to follow him – this important mandate is sometimes forgotten by those seeking to serve God either in ordained ministry or in other ways. Before anything else, the fishermen had first to put aside their everyday concerns and preoccupations and devote themselves to following Jesus. There will be sacrifices to be made – priorities may have to be changed, values altered. For some, the whole direction of a life may have to change. The labyrinth is a useful symbol of this turning about, for once one has arrived at the centre of the labyrinth the only way to arrive at the outside again is to turn around – 180 degrees.

Reflection 1

You will need cards printed with some or all of the following quotations:
   'I am the way, the truth and the life.'
   'Follow me.'
   'For God so loved the world he gave his only son.'
   'I am the good shepherd.'
   'Love the Lord your God with all your heart and all your mind and all your soul.'

Take a card and walk with it into the labyrinth. Allow the phrase to sink into your consciousness, and to fill your whole being. Meditate on the phrase, repeat it, chant it. At the centre, pause, and then, if you feel able, place the card on to the ground as a token of your willingness to follow Christ wherever he may lead you. Turn around and take the path out.

Talk 2

> After this the Lord appointed seventy others and sent
> them on ahead of him in pairs to every town and place
> where he himself intended to go. He said to them, 'The
> harvest is plentiful, but the labourers are few; therefore
> ask the Lord of the harvest to send out labourers into
> his harvest. Go on your way. See, I am sending you out
> like lambs into the midst of wolves. Carry no purse, no
> bag, no sandals; and greet no one on the road.
> *Luke 10.1–4* (NIV)

One of the most challenging things about going on a
journey is the question of what to pack. If one is going
on pilgrimage, and carrying everything on one's back, it
is even more critical. The truth of the matter is that we
need less than we think – often, indeed, the contingencies
we pack for are sparked off by the weight of the things
we pack! One of the things that prevents Christians from
living a generous life is a sense that we need so many
things ourselves that we can't really spare anything for
anyone else. We need all of our time to sort out our own
things; we need to make lots of money or achieve many
things so that others will take us seriously; and we need
a safety net of goods and possessions in case things go
wrong. The Gospel text challenges everything we think
we need to be effective people of God. Jesus sends out his
ill-equipped, ill-educated people with nothing more than
a staff, a pair of shoes and a companion – that is all. They
had no qualifications and no certificates, yet they set out
to change the world – and they did. The concept of not
needing to be perfect in every way before we set out to do
the works of God is a vital one to grasp in our journey

of discipleship. In truth, all we need is an awareness of God's grace and a willingness to witness to his amazing love.

Reflection 2

You will need a set of cards for each participant with the following words or, better still, images from newspapers or magazines that represent these things:
  Money.
  Possessions.
  Status.
  Guilt.
  Lack of qualifications.
  Lack of confidence.
  Lack of time.
  Love.

Place all but the cards saying 'love' on the outside of the labyrinth. The cards bearing the word or image for 'love' need to go in a small pile in the centre.

Take a set of cards and shuffle them. As you walk through the labyrinth, study a different card at various intervals. Reflect on what the word or words on the card mean to you and how much of what they represent interferes with your ability to fulfil your vocation. When you reach the centre, pause and ask God for the grace to replace all your anxieties and obstacles with one simple word – love. Pick up a card with the word (or image of) 'love' and allow God's love to fill your heart, soul and mind, equipping you with all that is necessary to fulfil your potential as a child of God.

Talk 3

Now an angel of the Lord said to Philip, 'Go south to the road – the desert road – that goes down from Jerusalem to Gaza.' So he started out, and on his way he met an Ethiopian eunuch, an important official in charge of all the treasury of the Kandake (which means 'queen of the Ethiopians'). This man had gone to Jerusalem to worship, and on his way home was sitting in his chariot reading the Book of Isaiah the prophet. The Spirit told Philip, 'Go to that chariot and stay near it.' Then Philip ran up to the chariot and heard the man reading Isaiah the prophet. 'Do you understand what you are reading?' Philip asked. 'How can I,' he said, 'unless someone explains it to me?' So he invited Philip to come up and sit with him. This is the passage of Scripture the eunuch was reading:

'He was led like a sheep to the slaughter,
and as a lamb before its shearer is silent,
so he did not open his mouth.
In his humiliation he was deprived of justice.
Who can speak of his descendants?
For his life was taken from the earth.'

The eunuch asked Philip, 'Tell me, please, who is the prophet talking about, himself or someone else?' Then Philip began with that very passage of Scripture and told him the good news about Jesus. As they travelled along the road, they came to some water and the eunuch said, 'Look, here is water. What can stand in the way of my being baptised?' And he gave orders to stop the chariot. Then both Philip and the eunuch went down into the water and Philip baptised him. When

they came up out of the water, the Spirit of the Lord
suddenly took Philip away, and the eunuch did not see
him again, but went on his way rejoicing. Philip, however, appeared at Azotus and travelled about, preaching
the gospel in all the towns until he reached Caesarea.
Acts 8.26–40 (NIV)

This New Testament story has in it two elements that we
don't often meet in our daily life nowadays – chariots
and eunuchs. None the less, its immediacy and relevance
practically shouts off the page at us. We first meet the
eunuch reading Isaiah in his chariot, and the Spirit tells
Philip to go over to the chariot and join it. Philip listens to
the Spirit and acts on its prompting. So too must we listen
when prompted by the Spirit to share God's love with
those we meet. It is vital that all of us talk about our faith.
It isn't easy, but if we don't – who will? As that famous
saying goes – you are the only Bible many people will
ever read. Just let's make sure people see Christ working
in our lives.

Notice too that Philip does not wait for the eunuch to
approach him, but goes up and joins in with what he is
doing and then begins to talk. Seekers now do not want
or need someone telling them what is what. They need
someone to walk alongside them, accompanying them on
their journey of discovery. Our role as Christians who
wish to share the gospel is to strip away unimportant
fuss that is unnecessary to basic essentials. Once we have
decided on these essentials, we need to hold true to them
– not in a dogmatic or directive way, but with a spirit of
compassion, showing love to others as we ourselves are
loved.

Reflection 3

You will need paper footprints and pencils or pens. You can buy post-it notes in the shape of feet, or find templates from the internet to cut them out.

Before you enter the labyrinth, spend some time reflecting on the people who have led you to this point in your spiritual journey. They may be your parents or teachers, a member of the clergy, or perhaps the author of a book or a particular character in the Bible. Write each name on a footprint – you can write as many as you like. Try to put them in some sort of order – either chronological or in order of significance and importance. As you walk through the labyrinth, you may want to place these feet on the pathways, pausing each time to pray for the person named on the footprint. Alternatively, you may wish to place them in the centre, giving thanks for the impact that they have had on your life.

On your journey out of the labyrinth, think of the many ways in which your life can be an example to those around you – whether in offering hospitality, helping in the community, or simply being a witness to Christ among the people with whom you spend your life.

Workshop outline 5: Creative responses to the labyrinth

Introduction

Research on the activity of the human brain has discovered that when a subject walks the labyrinth, it is the right-hand side of the brain that is energized. This is the side of the brain that connects with the creative, intuitive, spontaneous actions and reactions of human beings – the left side being the source of logical, rational and calculated activities. It would follow from this, therefore, that walking the labyrinth enables our more creative side room to expand and flourish and that, from the act of walking, further creative responses can be elicited in a relaxed and spontaneous way.

The aim of this workshop is to encourage such creativity and artistry. It is not designed for professional artists or even those working in creative fields such as writing or design. It offers instead a safe place for ordinary people to explore a side to their personality and character that may normally lie dormant. Those whose daily lives are concerned with the concrete and the practical often welcome the chance to experiment with words and images. Equally, those whose lives are mainly occupied with cerebral matters can find new interest and enthusiasm for the tangible and sensory through interaction with material crafts.

This workshop differs slightly from the others in that the labyrinth walk comes sooner in the day. This is to enable sufficient time for participants to relax into a creative response after the walk.

The broad outline of a workshop is obviously completely up to the leader but, allowing time for worship,

introductions, breaks and labyrinth walking, the timetable usually ends up looking something like this:

10.00 a.m. – Gathering and worship

10.20 a.m. – Introductions
You might include a brief resumé of your career and
how you became interested in labyrinths. Use this time
also to discover the level of previous engagement of the
participants with the labyrinth, so that you can adjust
the rest of your material accordingly.

Include any housekeeping notices, such as refreshment provision and location of toilets.

10.45 a.m. –12.45 p.m. – Walking the labyrinth
The content of this session will depend on the experience of your participants and the size of the labyrinth
to be walked. It is easiest to calculate back from the end
time (12.45), to allow enough time for the walk, and
then use the remaining time for an introduction to the
labyrinth, questions, and ideally some time for group
reflection after the walk.

12.45–1.30 p.m. – Lunch
Encourage participants to move out of the labyrinth
area, to give themselves a chance to rest and to evaluate
what they have been experiencing.

*1.30–2.00 p.m. – Creative responses to the labyrinth –
introduction*
Include a brief description of each of the creative
responses available. Reassure participants that their
work will not be scrutinized or judged by others, and
that skill levels are irrelevant.

2.00–3.00 p.m. – Creative responses – practical

3.00–3.30 p.m. – Plenary session
Participants can be invited to share their experiences and show their crafts if they wish. Reflections on the whole day can be offered here.

3.30–4.00 p.m. – Closing worship and tea

As with all the workshops, it is essential to ensure that the creative activities you are proposing are suitable for the group you are working with. This is particularly the case with this workshop – there are some institutions, for example, where scissors or sharp objects may be problematic, and others where the level of dexterity required for some of the craft activities may be beyond the capabilities of the workshop attendees. In fact, it is always a good idea to keep an open mind as to what level of creativity will be sparked by the labyrinth, and to what degree of skill the participants will engage with the activities. In one women's group I was surprised by the great difficulty experienced with a simple sewing project, and equally surprised at the ingenuity and artistry with which they worked with the clay that was also offered.

It is a good idea to offer a wide range of crafts at different levels of ability – very often workshop participants will begin with an easy craft such as colouring in a picture of the labyrinth. It is only when they have gained some confidence in their abilities that they will feel able to move on to something more challenging. It is important also to stress that this workshop is not a competition and that the crafts are not going to be put on display. All creative activities are simply for the benefit of those who are engaging in them, and after the event they will be free to take them away or dispose of them as they wish. A large dustbin bag should be provided for this at the beginning of the workshop, so that 'failed' attempts can be quietly binned; however, participants should be encouraged not to view their efforts as failures, but simply, as with the labyrinth, as steps along the way, valuable in that they enable the creator to progress towards their centre.

Below are listed a few crafts that can be used in the context of a creative response to labyrinth walking. These emphasize the unicursal nature of the labyrinth and are aimed at new walkers in that the crafts help them to understand the nature and design of a labyrinth through working on their own.

Materials

This workshop is unusual in that it will require a significant amount of equipment – another factor to consider when offering this to outside groups. Public transport becomes problematic if you are weighed down with blocks of clay and rolls of paper!

Each craft suggested below has its own materials list, but some general ones include:

Crayons and felt-tipped pens.

Good-quality paper, ideally A5 size, in an appealing colour – this can often be less daunting and more writer-friendly than large sheets of expectant A4.

Scissors.

Some large sheets of A3 paper, both coloured and plain.

Glue sticks.

Creative response: Labyrinth colouring

You will need labyrinth patterns, felt-tipped pens and crayons.

For some adults, it can be very challenging to be asked to engage in creative activities that they may have stopped doing when they were children. The safety of colouring in, and the attractive effects that can easily be achieved, can be reassuring to the nervous participant – hopefully giving confidence to try a more complicated activity. For adults and children alike, the simple act of colouring in a labyrinth can be both calming and satisfying.

Labyrinth patterns can be downloaded copyright free from Wikimedia Commons (commons.wikimedia.org). Simply enter 'labyrinth' in the search box and a variety of labyrinth patterns will be found, which can easily be printed on to A4 paper. As a variation on these, Celtic patterns, with their sinuous curving lines which twist and turn in complex patterns, can also be offered. These can also help participants think of other labyrinth patterns that they encounter in their daily lives, and the effect these might have. Copyright-free Celtic patterns are less easy to find on the internet – a safer bet might be to use ready-printed ones such as those offered by craft sites. Here you can purchase quite cheaply sets of colouring cards and decorations.

Plain pieces of paper can also be provided and participants encouraged to draw and design their own patterns, incorporating areas for reflection or different shapes of path, etc. A guide on how to draw a simple classic-style labyrinth can be downloaded from Wikimedia Commons.

Creative response: Writing

You will need attractive sheets of A5 paper, a variety of pens, pencils and crayons.

In a similar way, paper and writing implements should be offered to enable workshop participants to journal their feelings and express their experiences on the labyrinth in writing or poetry. For some, this may be an easy task – others may find it challenging to express personal emotions in writing. Reassure them that these works are personal and private and will not be scrutinized by others unless invited to do so. If the participants seem only to use words, encourage them to add illustrations or patterns to interact with other areas of their imagination and creativity.

Creative response: God's eye weavings

You will need small wooden craft sticks, glue gun, lengths of coloured wool and scissors.

God's eye weavings are ancient spiritual objects associated mainly with the peoples of the Americas. They were often made in celebration or blessing, being presented as gifts for a new home or to protect people during a hazardous trail through the wilderness. They are supposed to represent a faith in the all-seeing nature of God. Their use of a continuous length of coloured thread around a central cross design makes them a suitable craft for a celebration of the unicursal nature of the labyrinth.

For most workshops, it is advisable to do the preparatory work – that of sticking together two craft sticks in the shape of an equal-sided cross – beforehand. Although working with an object from the beginning is a good idea, glue guns introduce a level of hazard and mess that is often not practical.

Once you have your cross, cut a fairly long piece of wool – not so long that it gets tangled up, but not so short that new strands need to be fastened on every two minutes. Tie the wool on to the centre of the cross, then wind it diagonally from left to right over the central part of the cross, then right to left, until the middle is covered. Once you are satisfied that the wool is firmly fastened and the centre is covered, you can begin weaving. Take the wool behind the top arm and then back over the front of the top arm. Then, working anticlockwise, take the wool behind the left arm then back over the front of the left arm, behind the bottom arm and back over, and finally behind the right arm then back over the front to complete one round. Continue until the cross is as filled in as you want it to be. Join new thread by knotting on at the back of the cross. Finish by wrapping the wool down one arm and knotting.

Creative response: Clay

You will need blocks of air-drying clay, shaping and modelling tools, and protective cloth.

Working with clay can be enormously satisfying; its smooth texture is appealing and moulding and shaping the clay can be very relaxing. An additional appeal lies in the fact that mistakes can be quickly remoulded! Encourage participants to model their response in any way they please – some people will want to make model labyrinths, using either raised coils of clay as the path or drawing the lines into a slab of clay. Others might want to make an impression of the thoughts and feelings that occurred to them while on the walk.

Air-drying clay is easiest on these occasions as the models need no further work. Ensure that surfaces are protected and that there is provision for hand-washing afterwards.

Creative response: Collage

You will need strong A3 paper or thin card, PVA glue, crayons, felt-tipped pens, paints, scissors and brushes.

If the labyrinth is an outdoor one, this can be a collage using natural objects gathered on or near the path, either reproducing the pattern of the labyrinth itself or simply celebrating its place in the landscape. Once again, many adult participants will not have done anything like this since their childhood and may be nervous of committing their artistic efforts to paper. Reassurance is needed that nothing has to be glued down, and that all efforts can be binned at the end of the session – although this rarely happens in fact!

Creative response: Sand labyrinths

You will need shallow trays of dry sand, pebbles, shells, beads, sticks, etc., for making patterns.

Many craft shops sell shallow lidded boxes that are ideal for a thin layer of sand in which patterns can be drawn and decorated, or which participants can simply allow to run through their fingers, enjoying the texture and watching the shapes it makes as it falls. This simple craft has no actual end product, but serves as a further meditation device or a place to experiment with labyrinth patterns and designs before committing them to paper and clay.

Creative response: Virtual labyrinths

You will need beads, bead thread, a large bead cross-shaped pendant, and scissors.

Instructions on how to make a virtual labyrinth are found in the Appendix. Providing the materials to enable the participants to make their own virtual labyrinths will encourage a good understanding of how it works, although very close attention must be paid as even one bead in the wrong place makes the whole walk wrong!

Creative response workshop: Suggestion for worship

GATHERING

As the light of a new day shines upon us, we thank the Creator God for the love he has poured into the work of his hands:

Most High, all-powerful, good God
All praises be yours, all glory all honour and all
    blessing.
To you alone Most High do they belong.
No mortal lips are worthy to pronounce your name.
All praise be yours with all your creatures.
(Canticle of the Sun, St Francis of Assisi, c. 1181–1226)

Gracious God, help us to be mindful of your presence
today.
Guide us through its events and encounters,
Bless our words and our actions,
Help us to see your face in the face of those we meet and
Give us the grace to begin, engage with
And end this day in your love and truthfulness. **Amen**

CONFESSION

We remember those times when we have spoiled the
works of God, when our thoughts, words or actions have
marred and damaged our environment, our fellow human
beings and ourselves. Forgive us, Lord, for those times
when we have not honoured your creation, make whole
that which we have injured, and enable us to journey
onwards in your path.

Silence

Father, forgive us.

ABSOLUTION

God saw all that he had made, and it was very good. And
there was evening and there was morning – the sixth day.
Thus the heavens and the earth were created in all their
vast array. The Lord God took the man and put him in
the Garden of Eden to work it and take care of it.

Help us to take our place as your people in your world
again, through the grace of your Son, Jesus Christ. **Amen**

OLD TESTAMENT READING

The LORD said to Moses, 'Tell the Israelites to bring me an offering. You are to receive the offering for me from everyone whose heart prompts them to give. These are the offerings you are to receive from them: gold, silver and bronze; blue, purple and scarlet yarn and fine linen; goat hair; ram skins dyed red and another type of durable leather; acacia wood; olive oil for the light; spices for the anointing oil and for the fragrant incense; and onyx stones and other gems to be mounted on the ephod and breastpiece. Then let them make a sanctuary for me, and I will dwell among them. Make this tabernacle and all its furnishings exactly like the pattern I will show you.
Exodus 25.1–9 (NIV)

NEW TESTAMENT READING

From Troas we put out to sea and sailed straight for Samothrace, and the next day we went on to Neapolis. From there we travelled to Philippi, a Roman colony and the leading city of that district of Macedonia. And we stayed there several days. On the Sabbath we went outside the city gate to the river, where we expected to find a place of prayer. We sat down and began to speak to the women who had gathered there. One of those listening was a woman from the city of Thyatira named Lydia, a dealer in purple cloth. She was a worshipper of God. The Lord opened her heart to respond to Paul's message. When she and the members of her household were baptised, she invited us to her home. 'If

you consider me a believer in the Lord,' she said, 'come and stay at my house.' And she persuaded us.
Acts 16.11–15 (NIV)

Silence

PRAYERS

Creator God, the earth and all that is in it was lovingly made by you. Help us to rejoice in its beauties and make us responsible stewards of its glories. Give us the grace to see the infinite possibilities of your love in the tiniest piece of your creation – a seed, a pebble, a young animal, a child. Help us to realize our own potential for creating works of beauty and grace, not just with our hands, but with our hearts and minds as well, so that the whole of our being is in harmony with your will, and we become more fully the people you intend us to be. **Amen**

Loving God, our lives often seem broken or damaged, scarred and chipped by the actions of ourselves and others. Take our brokenness and heal it with your love, creating a thing of beauty from the scattered images of ourselves, as a mosaic turns broken pieces of pottery into an image that is perfect in its wholeness. **Amen**

4

Ideas and Outlines for Worship

Introduction

Using the labyrinth in traditional services can often be seen as too new and challenging for a church to undertake. However, there are many ways in which a labyrinth walk can be incorporated into a regular church service without disrupting the flow of the liturgy or the engagement of the congregation. The following are suggestions for ways in which a labyrinth walk can be used in seasonal and special services. There are many liturgies available for such services and these will not be duplicated here; this section simply offers notes on appropriate themes and readings which will, together with the labyrinth walk, enhance the meaning of the festival being celebrated, or add another dimension to it.

The arrangement of the building for the service will depend upon the size of the labyrinth and how it fits into the space available. It is a good idea, however, to ensure that the labyrinth is in full view, ideally with chairs arranged all around its exterior, leaving a space at the entrance. Pens and paper should be freely available, and members of the congregation encouraged to journal their reflections and responses as they wait for others to complete their walk. It should be emphasized, however, that this is voluntary.

Worship event
ADVENT

Advent is the beginning of the church year, but it occurs when the season of winter is gaining strength. The nights are getting longer, the weather can be very unpleasant, and there is a strong temptation to find comfort in a mental and spiritual hibernation until the worst of the winter is over. But Advent is a time for watching and waiting for signs of the coming of God's kingdom, and for heralding those signs to those around us. And just as we watch for the coming of the hope of the world in the birth of Christ, so we remember that God patiently and faithfully watches over us.

OPENING

I wait for the Lord, my whole being waits
And in his word I put my hope.

We have gathered to watch for the signs of the kingdom, to keep ourselves awake in the company of others seeking the Advent hope. We look through the darkness for signs of the coming light, and trust that the one who watches over our watching will be revealed in glory.

Merciful God, we wait in hope for your kingdom. Help us to see the signs of its coming in the words and works of those around us. Give us the grace also to be a sign of hope to others.

SUGGESTED READINGS

How beautiful on the mountains are the feet of those
who bring good news, who proclaim peace, who bring
good tidings, who proclaim salvation, who say to
Zion, 'Your God reigns!' Listen, your watchmen lift
up their voices; together they shout for joy. When the
LORD returns to Zion, they will see it with their own
eyes. Burst into songs of joy together, you ruins of Jerusalem, for the LORD has comforted his people, he has
redeemed Jerusalem. The LORD will lay bare his holy
arm in the sight of all the nations, and all the ends of
the earth will see the salvation of our God.
Isaiah 52.7–10 (NIV)

You, God, are my God, earnestly I seek you;
I thirst for you, my whole being longs for you,
in a dry and parched land where there is no water.
I have seen you in the sanctuary
and beheld your power and your glory.
Because your love is better than life,
my lips will glorify you.
I will praise you as long as I live,
and in your name I will lift up my hands.
I will be satisfied as with the richest of foods;
with singing lips my mouth will praise you.
On my bed I remember you;
I think of you through the watches of the night.
Because you are my help,
I sing in the shadow of your wings.
I cling to you; your right hand upholds me.
Psalm 63.1–8 (NIV)

At that time the kingdom of heaven will be like ten virgins who took their lamps and went out to meet the bridegroom. Five of them were foolish and five were wise. The foolish ones took their lamps but did not take any oil with them. The wise ones, however, took oil in jars along with their lamps. The bridegroom was a long time in coming, and they all became drowsy and fell asleep. At midnight the cry rang out: 'Here's the bridegroom! Come out to meet him!' Then all the virgins woke up and trimmed their lamps. The foolish ones said to the wise, 'Give us some of your oil; our lamps are going out.' 'No,' they replied, 'there may not be enough for both us and you. Instead, go to those who sell oil and buy some for yourselves.' But while they were on their way to buy the oil, the bridegroom arrived. The virgins who were ready went in with him to the wedding banquet. And the door was shut. Later the others also came. 'Lord, Lord,' they said, 'open the door for us!' But he replied, 'Truly I tell you, I don't know you.'

Therefore keep watch, because you do not know the day or the hour.
Matthew 25.1–13 (NIV)

LABYRINTH ACTIVITY

You will need a basket containing bulbs at the entrance to the labyrinth, and pots containing potting compost in the centre, on some plastic sheeting if need be.

Invite walkers to take a bulb and walk into the centre. The bulb contains new life within it so it should be held with love; however, at the moment its appearance is lifeless and unattractive.

Each walker should plant their bulb in a pot, then walk out carrying it. The bulb is now completely hidden – no one can see what the pot contains. But soon roots will find their way through the soil, and the first tip of green will be seen above the surface. Often the first signs of hope and growth are small and easily missed – only by being very observant can we spot them. Encourage walkers to consider also how they carry this new growth – so too must Christians carry hope to others.

PRAYERS

In the tender mercy of our God, the dayspring from on high shall break upon us, to give light to those who dwell in darkness and in the shadow of death and to guide our feet into the way of peace.

Lord, we pray for the coming of peace among our nations, our communities, our families and in our hearts. We pray for the return of righteousness and justice in all the world, and we commit ourselves to working for these things as far as we are able. We ask for the grace to stay faithful and watchful in these dark times, confident in the coming of your kingdom.

> Stir up, we beseech thee, O Lord, the wills of thy faithful people; that they, plenteously bringing forth the fruit of good works, may of thee be plenteously rewarded; through Jesus Christ our Lord. **Amen**
> *Collect for Trinity 25, BCP*

CLOSING

You gave me life and showed me kindness
And in your providence watched over my spirit.

Only be careful, and watch yourselves closely so that
you do not forget the things your eyes have seen or let
them fade from your heart as long as you live.
Deuteronomy 4.9 (NIV)

Worship event
ALL SOULS

All Souls occurs on 2 November, and around that time many churches offer commemoration services to remember those who have died; mourning their passing, celebrating their lives, and praying for their souls. This theme is followed here, with a focus on giving thanks for all that the loved one brought to their family and their community, and to dedicating ourselves to continuing their work of love and service.

OPENING

Blessed are they that mourn
For they shall be comforted.

We have gathered together to remember those who have walked the path from this world into the next, to thank God for their lives and to commit ourselves to living in such a way that their legacy of love is preserved and shared with those who follow.

Loving Father, we thank you for the gift of life,
even as we mourn those whom we see no longer.
Help us to be aware of your presence with us
as we remember those we loved
and to trust in your saving love
that extends beyond this life into eternity. **Amen**

SUGGESTED READINGS

I called to the LORD out of my distress, and he answered me; out of the belly of Sheol I cried, and you heard my voice. You cast me into the deep, into the heart of the seas, and the flood surrounded me; all your waves and your billows passed over me. Then I said, 'I am driven away from your sight; how shall I look again upon your holy temple?' The waters closed in over me; the deep surrounded me; weeds were wrapped around my head at the roots of the mountains. I went down to the land whose bars closed upon me for ever; yet you brought up my life from the Pit, O LORD my God. As my life was ebbing away, I remembered the LORD; and my prayer came to you, into your holy temple. Those who worship vain idols forsake their true loyalty. But I with the voice of thanksgiving will sacrifice to you; what I have vowed I will pay. Deliverance belongs to the LORD!

Jonah 2.2–9 (NRSV)

How lovely is your dwelling-place,
O LORD of hosts!
My soul longs, indeed it faints
for the courts of the LORD;
my heart and my flesh sing for joy
to the living God.

Even the sparrow finds a home,
and the swallow a nest for herself,
where she may lay her young,
at your altars, O LORD of hosts,
my King and my God.

Happy are those who live in your house,
ever singing your praise.

Happy are those whose strength is in you;
in whose heart are the highways to Zion.
Psalm 84.1–5 (NRSV)

Do not let your hearts be troubled. You believe in God;
believe also in me. My Father's house has many rooms;
if that were not so, would I have told you that I am
going there to prepare a place for you? And if I go and
prepare a place for you, I will come back and take you
to be with me that you also may be where I am. You
know the way to the place where I am going.' Thomas
said to him, 'Lord, we don't know where you are going,
so how can we know the way?' Jesus answered, 'I am
the way and the truth and the life. No one comes to the
Father except through me.
John 14.1–6 (NIV)

LABYRINTH ACTIVITY

*When the service is being advertised, ask the congregation to bring with them a photo of the person they are
remembering. For those who come without a photo, provide a selection of images including crosses, hearts and
flowers. These should be fairly small in size, no more than
3"/10cm square.*

Ask the congregation to walk into the centre of the labyrinth holding the photo and focusing on what the person
meant to them. Encourage them to remember happy times
and the good qualities of the deceased.

In the middle of the labyrinth, if there is room, set a small table covered with a purple cloth, with a cross standing on it. As each walker reaches the centre, they can place their photo at the foot of the cross. As they do so, encourage them to let go of their anxiety concerning this person, as well as any feelings of residual guilt or unease concerning their relationship.

On the journey out of the labyrinth, consider the qualities of the deceased that should be carried forward into the future, and the ways in which their love can be maintained and flourish.

Once everyone has finished the walk, a few moments' silence should follow.

CLOSING

Then I [John] saw a new heaven and a new earth; for the first heaven and the first earth had passed away, and the sea was no more. And I saw the holy city, the new Jerusalem, coming down out of heaven from God, prepared as a bride adorned for her husband. And I heard a loud voice from the throne saying, 'See, the home of God is among mortals. He will dwell with them; they will be his peoples, and God himself will be with them; he will wipe every tear from their eyes. Death will be no more; mourning and crying and pain will be no more, for the first things have passed away.' And the one who was seated on the throne said, 'See, I am making all things new.' Also he said, 'Write this, for these words are trustworthy and true.' Then he said to me, 'It is done! I am the Alpha and the Omega, the beginning and the end. To the thirsty I will give water as a gift from the spring of the water of life. Those who

conquer will inherit these things, and I will be their God and they will be my children.'
Revelation 21.1–7 (NRSV)

PRAYERS

Keep watch, dear Lord, with those who work, or watch, or weep this night,
and give your angels charge over those who sleep.
Tend the sick, give rest to the weary,
Sustain the dying, calm the suffering
And pity the distressed: all for your love's sake,
O Christ our redeemer.
Augustine of Hippo, 354–430

Bring us, O Lord God, at our last awakening, into the house and gate of heaven, to enter into that gate and dwell in that house, where there shall be no darkness nor dazzling, but one equal light; no noise nor silence, but one equal music; no fears nor hopes, but one equal possession; no ends nor beginnings but one equal eternity; in the habitations of thy Majesty and thy Glory, world without end. **Amen**
Adapted from John Donne, 1572–1631

We give back, to you, O God, those whom you gave to us. You did not lose them when you gave them to us, and we do not lose them by their return to you. Your dear Son has taught us that life is eternal and love cannot die. So death is only an horizon, and an horizon is only the limit of our sight. Open our eyes to see more clearly, and draw us closer to you that we may know that we are nearer to our loved ones, who

are with you. You have told us that you are preparing
a place for us: prepare us also for that happy place, that
where you are we may also be always, O dear Lord of
life and death.
William Penn, 1644–1718

Nunc Dimittis (The Song of Simeon)

Now, Lord, you let your servant go in peace:
your word has been fulfilled.

My own eyes have seen the salvation
which you have prepared in the sight of every people;

A light to reveal you to the nations
and the glory of your people Israel.

Glory to the Father and to the Son
and to the Holy Spirit;
as it was in the beginning is now
and shall be for ever. **Amen**
From Common Worship, *page 86*

Worship event
CANDLEMAS

The feast of Candlemas takes place on 2 February, 40 days after Christmas. It represents the turning point away from the celebration of Christmas towards the austerity of preparations for Lent. It also takes place during the gloomiest time of year, which makes its secondary purpose – that of blessing the year's supply of candles for the church – a powerful symbol of the light of Christ's love breaking forth into the darkness of this world. Candles remind us not only of Christ's love for us, but of our duty to shine as lights in the world, sharing God's love with those we meet.

OPENING

Behold the light of Christ
Come into our hearts, Lord Jesus.

Blessed light giver, life enhancer, world saviour! We gather to celebrate the breaking forth of your love and light into the world, shining into the dark places with your burning love. We commemorate the presentation of Christ in the temple, and as his parents dedicated his life to God, so we in our turn commit our lives to love and praise. Blessed be Father, Son and Holy Spirit for ever.

SUGGESTED READINGS

In the year that King Uzziah died, I saw the Lord, high and exalted, seated on a throne; and the train of his robe filled the temple. Above him were seraphim, each with six wings: with two wings they covered their

[81]

faces, with two they covered their feet, and with two they were flying. And they were calling to one another:

'Holy, holy, holy is the LORD Almighty;
the whole earth is full of his glory.'

At the sound of their voices the doorposts and thresholds shook and the temple was filled with smoke.

'Woe to me!' I cried. 'I am ruined! For I am a man of unclean lips, and I live among a people of unclean lips, and my eyes have seen the King, the LORD Almighty.'

Then one of the seraphim flew to me with a live coal in his hand, which he had taken with tongs from the altar. With it he touched my mouth and said, 'See, this has touched your lips; your guilt is taken away and your sin atoned for.'

Then I heard the voice of the Lord saying, 'Whom shall I send? And who will go for us?'

And I said, 'Here am I. Send me.'
Isaiah 6.1–8 (NIV)

The earth is the LORD's and all that is in it,
the world, and those who live in it;
for he has founded it on the seas,
and established it on the rivers.
Who shall ascend the hill of the LORD?
And who shall stand in his holy place?
Those who have clean hands and pure hearts,
who do not lift up their souls to what is false,
and do not swear deceitfully.
They will receive blessing from the LORD,
and vindication from the God of their salvation.
Such is the company of those who seek him,
who seek the face of the God of Jacob.

Lift up your heads, O gates! and be lifted up, O
   ancient doors! that the King of glory may come in.
Who is the King of glory? The LORD, strong and
   mighty, the LORD, mighty in battle.
Lift up your heads, O gates! and be lifted up, O
   ancient doors! that the King of glory may come in.
Who is this King of glory? The LORD of hosts, he is
   the King of glory.
Psalm 24 (NIV)

When the time came for their purification according to
the law of Moses, they brought him up to Jerusalem to
present him to the Lord (as it is written in the law of
the Lord, 'Every firstborn male shall be designated as
holy to the Lord'), and they offered a sacrifice according to what is stated in the law of the Lord, 'a pair of
turtle-doves or two young pigeons.'

   Now there was a man in Jerusalem whose name was
Simeon; this man was righteous and devout, looking
forward to the consolation of Israel, and the Holy Spirit
rested on him. It had been revealed to him by the Holy
Spirit that he would not see death before he had seen the
Lord's Messiah. Guided by the Spirit, Simeon came into
the temple; and when the parents brought in the child
Jesus, to do for him what was customary under the law,
Simeon took him in his arms and praised God, saying,

   'Master, now you are dismissing your servant in
     peace,
   according to your word;
   for my eyes have seen your salvation,
   which you have prepared in the presence of all
     peoples,

a light for revelation to the Gentiles
and for glory to your people Israel.'

And the child's father and mother were amazed at
what was being said about him. Then Simeon blessed
them and said to his mother Mary, 'This child is des-
tined for the falling and the rising of many in Israel,
and to be a sign that will be opposed so that the inner
thoughts of many will be revealed – and a sword will
pierce your own soul too.'

There was also a prophet, Anna the daughter of
Phanuel, of the tribe of Asher. She was of a great age,
having lived with her husband for seven years after her
marriage, then as a widow to the age of eighty-four.
She never left the temple but worshipped there with
fasting and prayer night and day. At that moment she
came, and began to praise God and to speak about the
child to all who were looking for the redemption of
Jerusalem.

When they had finished everything required by the
law of the Lord, they returned to Galilee, to their own
town of Nazareth. The child grew and became strong,
filled with wisdom; and the favour of God was upon
him.

Luke 2.22–40 (NRSV)

LABYRINTH ACTIVITY

A basket of unlit candles should be provided at the entrance to the labyrinth and a lit Paschal candle or saved Advent wreath at the centre.

This activity is most powerful if it takes place in the late afternoon or evening, when the venue can be quite dark and the light from the candles even more striking.

The labyrinth will look quite spectacular if it is circled by candles – either traditional tealights or, if the labyrinth is canvas or vulnerable to wax damage, electric tealights can now be purchased reasonably cheaply from large supermarkets and have quite a long battery time.

The Advent wreath or Paschal candle will signify that Candlemas is a turning point in the year, when the Christmas cycle has ended and we turn towards Lent; and they also symbolize the prophecies concerning Christ as the light of the world, reflecting the words and actions of Simeon and Anna.

Invite people to take an unlit candle as they walk in and light it from the symbolic light of Christ in the centre. The journey into the centre of the labyrinth could be focused on prayers for the dark places of the world, while the journey outwards with the lit candle can be directed towards meditation on ways in which the walker can act as a light of Christ in their own community.

PRAYERS

Lord, giver of light
Shine in the darkness of this world

Lord, bringer of hope
Help us to bring hope to others

Lord, sender of love
Give us the grace both to receive your love and to share
it with others.

As the hopes of Simeon and Anna were fulfilled in Christ,
so may we fulfil your purposes for us, O Lord. May we be
light bringers and hope givers, so that we too may be sent
out into the world to reveal your glory.

> Christ be with me, Christ within me
> Christ behind me, Christ before me
> Christ beside me, Christ to win me
> Christ to comfort and restore me.
> Christ beneath me, Christ above me
> Christ in quiet, Christ in danger
> Christ in hearts of all that love me
> Christ in mouth of friend and stranger.
> *Patrick of Ireland, c. 385–461*

Worship event
ROGATIONTIDE

This festival was originally celebrated on the three week-days before Ascension, but more recently it has been moved to the Sunday before. It was traditionally the time of year when the young crops in the fields were blessed. It is also the occasion when the 'beating of the bounds' occurs – when members of a parish accompany the priest round the parish boundaries, praying for God's blessing on the parish and its crops. Today, Rogation Sunday is a good time to celebrate God's creation, rejoicing in its infinite variety, created with such love. We can also offer intercessions for the world, raising our hearts and minds above our own narrow horizons to contemplate the worldwide community.

Weather permitting, this is a service that is very suited to being held outside in some form of green space. It does not have to be woodland or open countryside – a park or even the church surroundings would also be quite appropriate. Before the service, select a site that will be suitable for constructing a full-size labyrinth. The simplest pattern to use is the classic three- or five-circuit labyrinth (see page 171). Once you have selected your site, make sure it is clear of debris and made as level and smooth as possible. Mark out the centre point of the labyrinth and the external points that must be joined by planting upright sticks or placing large stones at the points. If you are not confident that you can successfully create the pattern just from these points, then the entire outline of the labyrinth can be traced on the ground either marking the soil with a stick, or trailing sand or flour. Then gather a large pile of sticks, stones and foliage and place to one side of the site.

During the labyrinth activity part of the service, members of the congregation can be invited to help construct their own labyrinth using the materials provided. The congregation can then walk their own creation as part of the worship.

Alternatively, if the venue has to be inside, use a labyrinth that has already been created – either a canvas one or one marked out in masking tape, etc. Place a pile of sticks and other foliage at the entrance to the labyrinth. During the labyrinth activity section, walkers are invited to select something and then take it into the centre, examining it, getting to know it, becoming fully aware of its individuality and beauty. At the centre, place a large piece of paper and some glue so that a collage can be created. You might wish to draw some basic outlines of trees, etc. and define the sky and land spaces, but this is not obligatory.

If the venue is not conducive to this, place a simple drawing of the world at the centre of the labyrinth, then outline the paths with foam stickers of animals, birds, fish, flowers, etc. These can be bought in large tubs quite cheaply from craft stores. As the walkers proceed through the labyrinth, they can collect some of these stickers to decorate the map.

OPENING

You are worthy, our Lord and God,
to receive glory and honour and power
For you created all things,
and by your will they existed and were created.

Lord God, who has taught us only to ask and it will be given to us, we give you thanks for the beauties of your creation, and the love from which it sprang. We pray for nations and countries, that seedtime and harvest may endure until the coming of your kingdom on earth and the revelation of your true glory.

SUGGESTED READINGS

Then God said, 'I give you every seed-bearing plant on the face of the whole earth and every tree that has fruit with seed in it. They will be yours for food. And to all the beasts of the earth and all the birds in the sky and all the creatures that move along the ground – everything that has the breath of life in it – I give every green plant for food.' And it was so.

God saw all that he had made, and it was very good. And there was evening, and there was morning – the sixth day.
Genesis 1.29–31 (NIV)

Praise the LORD, my soul.
LORD my God, you are very great;
you are clothed with splendour and majesty.
The LORD wraps himself in light as with a garment;
he stretches out the heavens like a tent
and lays the beams of his upper chambers on their
　　waters.
He makes the clouds his chariot
and rides on the wings of the wind.
He makes winds his messengers,
flames of fire his servants.
He set the earth on its foundations;
it can never be moved …
He makes springs pour water into the ravines;

it flows between the mountains.
They give water to all the beasts of the field;
the wild donkeys quench their thirst.
The birds of the sky nest by the waters;
they sing among the branches.
He waters the mountains from his upper chambers;
the land is satisfied by the fruit of his work.
He makes grass grow for the cattle,
and plants for people to cultivate –
bringing forth food from the earth ...
May the glory of the LORD endure for ever;
may the LORD rejoice in his works –
he who looks at the earth, and it trembles,
who touches the mountains, and they smoke.
I will sing to the LORD all my life;
I will sing praise to my God as long as I live.
May my meditation be pleasing to him,
as I rejoice in the LORD.
But may sinners vanish from the earth
and the wicked be no more.
Praise the LORD, my soul.
Praise the LORD.
Psalm 104.1–5, 10–14, 31–35 (NIV)

For God so loved the world that he gave his one and
only Son, that whoever believes in him shall not perish
but have eternal life. For God did not send his Son into
the world to condemn the world, but to save the world
through him.
John 3.16–17 (NIV)

LABYRINTH ACTIVITY

Invite members of the congregation to walk the labyrinth, outside if weather permits or inside if not, as outlined on p. 88.

PRAYERS

Bountiful God,
You created all things, and rejoice in all that you have
    made.
Give us eyes and ears to see and hear the wonders of
    your creation,
And lips to tell others of the love you show through the
    beauty of all things.

> Lord, make me an instrument of your peace.
> Where there is hatred, let me sow love,
> Where there is injury, pardon,
> Where there is doubt, faith,
> Where there is despair, hope,
> Where there is darkness, light,
> Where there is sadness, joy.
> O divine Master, grant that I may not so much seek
> To be consoled as to console,
> To be understood as to understand,
> To be loved as to love.
> For it is in giving that we receive,
> It is in pardoning that we are pardoned,
> It is in dying that we are born to eternal life.
> *Anon., 20th century*

Deep peace of the running wave to you
Deep peace of the flowing air to you
Deep peace of the quiet earth to you
Deep peace of the shining stars to you
Deep peace of the shades of night to you
Moon and stars always giving light to you
Celtic prayer

CLOSING

Sow for yourselves righteousness; reap steadfast love;
   break up your fallow ground
**For it is time to seek the Lord, that he may come and
rain righteousness upon us.**

Go forth into the world in peace;
be of good courage;
hold fast that which is good;
render to no one evil for evil;
strengthen the fainthearted; support the weak;
help the afflicted; honour everyone;
love and serve the Lord,
, rejoicing in the power of the Holy Spirit.
From Common Worship

Worship event
PENTECOST

The feast of Pentecost occurs 50 days after Easter Sunday, and celebrates the descent of the Holy Spirit upon the disciples, enabling them to continue Christ's mission of a saving love full of faith and grace. For this reason it is often referred to as the birthday of the Church – though this service outline instead focuses on an offering of a person's whole self to the service of God. God seeks not just our minds or that part of them that we bring to church each week, but our hearts and bodies – everything that goes to make up the unique individual.

OPENING

We welcome the coming of the Holy Spirit
Let us glory in Christ Jesus in our service to God.

Heavenly Father, as we celebrate your gift to us of your Holy Spirit, we gather to dedicate our whole selves to your service. All that we are, all that we have, has been given to us by you, O Lord; help us to fulfil our potential as we work for the coming of your kingdom. **Amen**

SUGGESTED READINGS

But if serving the LORD seems undesirable to you, then choose for yourselves this day whom you will serve, whether the gods your ancestors served beyond the Euphrates, or the gods of the Amorites, in whose land you are living. But as for me and my household, we will serve the LORD.
Joshua 24.15 (NIV)

Come, let us sing for joy to the LORD; let us shout aloud
to the Rock of our salvation. Let us come before him
with thanksgiving and extol him with music and song.
For the LORD is the great God, the great King above all
gods. In his hand are the depths of the earth, and the
mountain peaks belong to him. The sea is his, for he
made it, and his hands formed the dry land. Come, let
us bow down in worship, let us kneel before the LORD
our Maker; for he is our God and we are the people of
his pasture, the flock under his care.
Psalm 95.1–7 (NIV)

For this reason, since the day we heard about you, we
have not stopped praying for you. We continually ask
God to fill you with the knowledge of his will through
all the wisdom and understanding that the Spirit gives,
so that you may live a life worthy of the LORD and
please him in every way: bearing fruit in every good
work, growing in the knowledge of God, being strength-
ened with all power according to his glorious might so
that you may have great endurance and patience, and
giving joyful thanks to the Father, who has qualified
you to share in the inheritance of his holy people in the
kingdom of light.
Colossians 1.9–12 (NIV)

LABYRINTH ACTIVITY

*This activity needs a sheet of paper for each participant,
one or more paint pads for handprints, glue sticks and
glitter. The paint pads should be red or gold, the traditional colours for Pentecost, symbolizing flames and the
Spirit. These can easily be obtained from art shops or*

places such as Hobbycraft, or from the internet. Hand-wipes should also be available.

After the readings, the congregation is invited to make two handprints on a piece of paper in the shape of a dove. This is done by overlapping the thumbs of each handprint to form the bird's body, with the rest of the fingers closed to make wings. This should be done in silence, and the congregation invited to return to their seats and look at the print they have made. The hands will all be different, and some will bear the marks of age, illness or injury. Handprints are all unique, just as we are in other ways. We bring different gifts and can serve God in many ways.

Invite people to walk the labyrinth holding their hand-prints, considering the gifts that have been given to them, and the ways in which they can serve God with them. If the labyrinth is properly protected, you can provide glue sticks and glitter in the centre. The handprint doves can then be sprinkled with glitter to symbolize the fire of the Spirit. The handprints can be left in the centre, or taken out again and kept.

PRAYERS

Teach us, O Lord,
To serve you as you deserve,
To give and not to count the cost,
To fight and not to heed the wounds,
To toil and not to seek for rest,
To labour and not to ask for any reward
Save that of knowing that we do your will.
Ignatius of Loyola, 1491–1556

Christ has no hands but our hands
To do his work today;
He has no feet but our feet
To lead men in his way;
He has no tongue but our tongue
To tell men how he died;
He has no help but our help
To bring them to his side.
Annie Johnson Flint, 1862–1932,
based on a prayer by Teresa of Avila, 1515–82

Help us, heavenly Father, to serve you in ways that both fulfil our potential and help to bring in your kingdom. Help us to avoid the pitfalls of idleness and busyness, of underestimating our gifts and of not using them fully. You know us completely; you know what we are capable of achieving in your service – give us the insight to know this also.

Worship event
LAMMASTIDE

Traditionally celebrated on or near 1 August, this ancient festival marks the start of the wheat harvest with a loaf of bread made from the new crop of wheat brought into church and blessed. It gives a good opportunity not merely for thankfulness for our physical food, but for commemorating the bread of life also.

OPENING

You, Lord, are the bread of heaven
Give us life.
We do not live by bread alone
Help us to feed on your word.

Great God, giver of all good things, you bring us seed-time and harvest, times for sowing and reaping. We come before you at the season of harvest time, giving thanks for the food we eat and mindful of those who have too little. We listen also to your words of wisdom and love, which feed our soul and make our hearts rejoice.

BLESSING OF THE LAMMASTIDE LOAF

Blessed are you, Lord God of all creation;
you bring forth bread from the fields
and give us the fruits of the earth in their seasons.
Accept this loaf, which we bring before you,
made from the harvest of your goodness.
Let it be for us a sign of your fatherly care.

Blessed are you, Lord our God,
worthy of our thanksgiving and praise.
From Common Worship: Times and Seasons, *page 619*

SUGGESTED READINGS

When the dew was gone, thin flakes like frost on the ground appeared on the desert floor. When the Israelites saw it, they said to each other, 'What is it?' For they did not know what it was.

Moses said to them, 'It is the bread the LORD has given you to eat. This is what the LORD has commanded: "Everyone is to gather as much as they need. Take an omer for each person you have in your tent."' The Israelites did as they were told; some gathered much, some little. And when they measured it by the omer, the one who gathered much did not have too much, and the one who gathered little did not have too little. Everyone had gathered just as much as they needed ... The people of Israel called the bread manna. It was white like coriander seed and tasted like wafers made with honey.
Exodus 16.14–18, 31 (NIV)

Give praise to the LORD, proclaim his name;
make known among the nations what he has done.
Sing to him, sing praise to him;
tell of all his wonderful acts.
Glory in his holy name;
let the hearts of those who seek the LORD rejoice.
Look to the LORD and his strength;
seek his face always.

Remember the wonders he has done,
his miracles, and the judgments he pronounced,
you his servants, the descendants of Abraham,
his chosen ones, the children of Jacob.
He is the LORD our God;
his judgments are in all the earth …

He brought out Israel, laden with silver and gold,
and from among their tribes no one faltered.
Egypt was glad when they left,
because dread of Israel had fallen on them.

He spread out a cloud as a covering,
and a fire to give light at night.
They asked, and he brought them quail;
he fed them well with the bread of heaven.
He opened the rock, and water gushed out;
it flowed like a river in the desert.

For he remembered his holy promise
given to his servant Abraham.
He brought out his people with rejoicing,
his chosen ones with shouts of joy;
he gave them the lands of the nations,
and they fell heir to what others had toiled for –
that they might keep his precepts and observe his laws.

Praise the LORD.
Psalm 105.1–7, 37–45 (NIV)

Jesus said to them, 'Very truly I tell you, it is not Moses
who has given you the bread from heaven, but it is my
Father who gives you the true bread from heaven. For
the bread of God is the bread that comes down from

heaven and gives life to the world.' 'Sir,' they said, 'always give us this bread.'

Then Jesus declared, 'I am the bread of life. Whoever comes to me will never go hungry, and whoever believes in me will never be thirsty.'
John 6.32–35 (NIV)

LABYRINTH ACTIVITY

Have two platters of different types of bread – matzos, pitta, whole grain, white sliced, etc. Place one at the entrance to the labyrinth and one at the centre.

Invite walkers to take a piece of bread and hold it in their hands as they walk. Encourage them to consider their attitude to food and drink – whether it is a generous and healthy one, aware of the plight of others, not greedy and thoughtless. Encourage them to meditate on whether they use food unwisely – either wastefully or as a comfort mechanism. Does food and drink control their lives?

In the centre, invite walkers to eat their piece of bread mindfully, savouring the taste, and giving thanks to God for its provision.

Worshippers can then take another piece of bread and walk out, this time meditating on Jesus, the bread of life. They might consider the ways in which God's word nourishes them, the amount of nourishment they seek, and what they do with it. Walkers can reflect on whether their focus should be directed more towards the spiritual bread than the physical, and how this change might come about.

Once they have returned to their seats, the second piece of bread can be eaten – again slowly and mindfully.

PRAYERS

God of ploughed earth and green shoots, Lord of ripening crops and golden grain, we rejoice in the signs of your goodness and bounty that surround us and marvel at your generosity. The simplest food is a complex gift containing all the wonders of creation, all the depths of your love; let it be a remembrance of your great sacrifice made for us. Let our eyes and minds never tire of the glories of the landscape, let our hearts and souls never cease to sing songs of praise and thankfulness.

Lord God, you are the source of all goodness – everything we have comes from you. Help us to see the signs of your kingdom in the world about us. Give us the grace to feed on the bread of life, which was given by you for all people. Help us to share our resources with those who have less than ourselves, and make us mindful always of their source.

CLOSING

May God the Father of our Lord Jesus Christ,
who is the source of all goodness and growth,
pour his blessing upon all things created,
and upon you his children,
that you may use his gifts to his glory and the welfare
  of all peoples.

Tend the earth, care for God's good creation
And bring forth the fruits of righteousness.
From Common Worship: Times and Seasons, *page 622*

Worship event
A SERVICE OF HOLY COMMUNION WITH LABYRINTH WALK

Celebrating the Eucharist on the labyrinth can be an immensely moving occasion; a worshipping community walking together along the same path, moving at their own individual pace, yet all held by the sacrifice of Christ within the sacred space of the labyrinth can be both intimate and at the same time give a glimpse of eternity.

OPENING

Wonderful and mysterious are your ways, O Lord
Help us to tread your paths in faith.

As we gather in the presence of God and in community with others, we place ourselves and our lives into the hands of God, trusting in his loving purposes for us. We offer ourselves completely to his service, content to be used by him in whatever ways are best for his kingdom. We are a chosen people, singled out by his great love to carry out his great commission and share the good news of salvation with those we meet.

SUGGESTED READINGS

It was not because you were more numerous than any other people that the LORD set his heart on you and chose you ... It was because the LORD loved you and kept the oath that he swore to your ancestors, that the LORD has brought you out with a mighty hand, and redeemed you from the house of slavery, from the hand of Pharaoh king of Egypt. Know therefore that the

LORD your God is God, the faithful God who maintains covenant loyalty with those who love him and keep his commandments, to a thousand generations.
Deuteronomy 7.7–9 (NRSV)

I call upon you, for you will answer me, O God;
incline your ear to me, hear my words.
Wondrously show your steadfast love,
O saviour of those who seek refuge
from their adversaries at your right hand.

Guard me as the apple of the eye;
hide me in the shadow of your wings …
Psalm 17.6–8 (NRSV)

Therefore I tell you, do not worry about your life, what you will eat or drink; or about your body, what you will wear. Is not life more than food, and the body more than clothes? Look at the birds of the air; they do not sow or reap or store away in barns, and yet your heavenly Father feeds them. Are you not much more valuable than they? Can any one of you by worrying add a single hour to your life?
Matthew 6.25–27 (NIV)

LABYRINTH ACTIVITY

Where and how to hold the labyrinth walk within the structure of the liturgy depends too much upon the nature of the labyrinth and the size of the congregation to allow many general assertions as to how best the labyrinth can be used. A congregation could gather round the outside of the labyrinth for the Liturgy of the Word and then begin the labyrinth walk at the Peace, arriving at the centre in time to receive communion. Alternatively, the walk could take place during the readings and intercessions, with the Peace being exchanged as the walkers move in and out of the labyrinth, and enabling the Eucharistic Prayer to take place at the altar if so desired. Alternatively, the altar could be placed in the centre, and the priest move outwards to distribute to a congregation gathered around the outside of the labyrinth. Members of a congregation could then walk after the distribution, perhaps arriving at the centre for the sending out.

If the labyrinth is small or the congregation too large to allow a walk to take place during the service, it could be used as a way of centring and focusing before the service begins.

One of the features of the labyrinth is the requirement simply to walk faithfully the path as it unfolds at the feet of the walker. This can be used to communicate the necessity for trusting in God's great love at all times in our lives, both the joyful and sorrowful occasions. Using relevant readings and prayers, the walk could take place instead of a sermon, with the congregation actually experiencing what it is to walk in the ways of the Lord, trusting in his loving purposes to guide us to our true destination.

PRAYER

My Father, I abandon myself to you.
Do with me as you will.
Whatever you may do with me, I thank you.
I am prepared for anything, I accept everything.
Provided your will is fulfilled in me, and in all
    creatures

I ask for nothing more, my God.
I place my soul in your hands.
I give it to you, my God,
With all the love of my heart
Because I love you.
And for me it is a necessity of love,
This gift of myself,
This placing of myself in your hands
Without reserve
In boundless confidence
Because you are my Father.
Charles de Foucauld, 1858–1916

CLOSING

God of our pilgrimage,
you have led us to the living water:
refresh and sustain us
as we go forward on our journey,
in the name of Jesus Christ our LORD.
*Post Communion for Trinity 6
(from* Common Worship, *page 411)*

May the road rise up to meet you
May the wind be always at your back
May the sun shine warm upon your face
May the rain fall softly upon your fields.
And until we meet again
May God hold you in the hollow of his hand.
Irish Blessing

Worship Event
HEALING SERVICE

A healing event can take place either at the end of a Eucharist, as part of a service of worship, or as a stand-alone event. Care must be taken when publicizing and introducing such occasions that expectations are not raised impossibly high. Especial care should be taken with the situation of the labyrinth for the walk – although dim lighting is atmospheric, it may be too dangerous in this context. Similarly, there should be plenty of seating available, and potential walkers reassured that if the walk is too demanding physically, they can ask for a chair to be placed where they are on the labyrinth so that they can rest before continuing, or simply leave the walk and reflect at the edge of the labyrinth.

OPENING

Blessed are those who have regard for the weak
The Lord delivers them in times of trouble.
The Lord protects and preserves them
They are counted among the blessed in the land.
Let us pray to the Father
For he knows what things we need.

Loving Christ, who walked among the wounded and sinful, help us to be aware of your healing presence among us now. Deliver us from the pains of mind, body and spirit, and help us to walk in wholeness in your paths.

SUGGESTED READINGS

But now, this is what the LORD says –
he who created you, Jacob,
he who formed you, Israel:
'Do not fear, for I have redeemed you;
I have summoned you by name; you are mine.
When you pass through the waters,
I will be with you;
and when you pass through the rivers,
they will not sweep over you.
When you walk through the fire,
you will not be burned;
the flames will not set you ablaze.
For I am the LORD your God,
the Holy One of Israel, your Saviour;
I give Egypt for your ransom,
Cush and Seba in your stead.
Since you are precious and honoured in my sight,
and because I love you,
I will give people in exchange for you,
nations in exchange for your life.
Isaiah 43.1–4 (NIV)

Praise the LORD, my soul;
all my inmost being, praise his holy name.
Praise the LORD, my soul,
and forget not all his benefits –
who forgives all your sins
and heals all your diseases,
who redeems your life from the pit
and crowns you with love and compassion,

who satisfies your desires with good things
so that your youth is renewed like the eagle's.

The LORD works righteousness
and justice for all the oppressed.

He made known his ways to Moses,
his deeds to the people of Israel:
the LORD is compassionate and gracious,
slow to anger, abounding in love.
He will not always accuse,
nor will he harbour his anger for ever;
he does not treat us as our sins deserve
or repay us according to our iniquities.
For as high as the heavens are above the earth,
so great is his love for those who fear him;
as far as the east is from the west,
so far has he removed our transgressions from us.

As a father has compassion on his children,
so the LORD has compassion on those who fear him;
for he knows how we are formed,
he remembers that we are dust.
The life of mortals is like grass,
they flourish like a flower of the field;
the wind blows over it and it is gone,
and its place remembers it no more.
But from everlasting to everlasting
the LORD's love is with those who fear him,
and his righteousness with their children's children –
with those who keep his covenant
and remember to obey his precepts.

The LORD has established his throne in heaven,
and his kingdom rules over all.
Praise the LORD, you his angels,
you mighty ones who do his bidding,
who obey his word.
Praise the LORD, all his heavenly hosts,
you his servants who do his will.
Praise the LORD, all his works
everywhere in his dominion.
Praise the LORD, my soul.
Psalm 103 (NIV)

Blessed are you who are poor,
for yours is the kingdom of God.
Blessed are you who hunger now,
for you will be satisfied.
Blessed are you who weep now,
for you will laugh.
Blessed are you when people hate you,
when they exclude you and insult you
and reject your name as evil,
because of the Son of Man.
Luke 6.20–22 (NIV)

LABYRINTH ACTIVITY

You will need oil for anointing.

It makes good sense to have the centre of the labyrinth
as the place where the oil of anointing and laying on of
hands should take place, unless the size of the labyrinth
or the number of the congregation prevents this. The
journey into the labyrinth could take place in silence,

with walkers praying for themselves and their concerns.
Before the anointing begins, as the first walker reaches the
centre, the following could be read:

> Is anyone among you ill? Let them call the elders of the
> church to pray over them and anoint them with oil in
> the name of the Lord. And the prayer offered in faith
> will make the sick person well; the Lord will raise them
> up. If they have sinned, they will be forgiven. Therefore
> confess your sins to each other and pray for each other
> so that you may be healed. The prayer of a righteous
> person is powerful and effective.
> *James 5.14–16* (NIV)

And for each person:

> 'In the name of God and trusting in his might alone,
> receive Christ's healing touch to make you whole. May
> Christ bring you wholeness of body, mind and spirit,
> deliver you from every evil, and give you his peace.'

As walkers leave the centre of the labyrinth and walk
past those still making their way in, they can be asked
to pray for those they pass, so that each member of the
congregation becomes involved in the act of intercession
for healing.

PRAYERS

> God of love, whose compassion never fails; we bring
> before thee the troubles and perils of people and nations,
> the sighing of prisoners and captives, the sorrows of the
> bereaved, the necessities of strangers, the helplessness
> of the weak, the despondency of the weary, the failing

powers of the aged. O Lord, draw near to each; for the sake of Jesus Christ our Lord.
St Anselm, c. 1033–1109

And I said to the man who stood at the gate of the year: 'Give me a light, that I may tread safely into the unknown!' And he replied: 'Go out into the darkness and put your hand into the Hand of God. That shall be to you better than light and safer than a known way.' So I went forth, and finding the Hand of God, trod gladly into the night ...
Minnie Louise Haskins, 1875–1957

CLOSING

Jesus says:

Peace I leave with you; my peace I give you. I do not give to you as the world gives. Do not let your hearts be troubled and do not be afraid.

John 14.27 (NIV)

5

Creative Ways of Using the Labyrinth with Children and Young People

Basic equipment

When introducing labyrinths to children and young people, it is very useful to have plenty of small labyrinth patterns available, so that the children can get a hands-on understanding of the single pathway. These can be photocopied from the internet – Wikimedia Commons provides copyright-free Chartres labyrinth patterns that are ideal for this purpose. For durability, make sure these are laminated. Shallow trays of sand can be provided for the children to try to trace the pattern – wooden chopsticks are good for this. A less potentially messy alternative is a number of A4 whiteboards and marker pens. As with any labyrinth walk, it is a good idea to have plenty of pens and a supply of paper available for those who are not actually walking to write down their thoughts and observations.

You might want to use some background music to encourage stillness and discourage chattering. This can be anything that is rhythmical and calming – classical music or Taizé chants are ideal.

Do not forget to bring a number of notices reminding pupils to remove their shoes before walking the labyrinth if this is necessary. You might also want to write a short notice encouraging walkers to be prepared to step aside to allow others to pass, and to keep as quiet as possible while walking to avoid disturbing other walkers. Occasionally, a period of quiet reflection such as a labyrinth walk will prove upsetting to a child, particularly if they are in a difficult or distressing personal situation. The calm of the labyrinth may bring their distress into clear focus and the result may be emotional. For these cases, rare though they are, a box of tissues, and a notice indicating the person to contact if the labyrinth walk proves upsetting or distressing, should be in plain sight.

General considerations

Although some of the subject suggestions listed below such as PSHE (personal, social and health education) might seem primarily for use within a school environment, the labyrinth can be used extremely successfully within a church context. Walking the labyrinth can introduce children to the topics of prayer and meditation, encouraging them to explore silence and reflection. As part of an organized activity such as Messy Church or Holiday Clubs, labyrinths can form the subject of several sessions, including outdoor activities, art and craft exercises, as well as encouraging the idea of a 'mini-pilgrimage'. The telling of well-known Bible stories can be given an extra zest by exploring them through the medium of labyrinths, and a journey round a church building can end with a labyrinth walk.

Wherever the location of the labyrinth, the most important principle for working with children and young people and the labyrinth is to ensure at all times the safety and security of those who walk it. There is usually some considerable degree of control over access to a church building, enabling you to plan a walk that is both safe and likely to be undisturbed by non-walkers. If a school building is being used, however, great care must be taken when considering where to site the labyrinth. The most obvious place would seem to be the school hall – it is probably the largest room in the school and will have ease of access. This can be an advantage if the labyrinth is to be made available at times other than specific teaching times, such as lunch breaks, to allow staff and pupils to walk the labyrinth in their own time and at their own pace. However, the very size of some halls can be off-putting – an individual can feel dwarfed and insecure by the large space, and the security offered by the space of the labyrinth can seem threatened. Again, if the labyrinth is placed in a very public place, this can be discouraging to those wishing to walk it in a degree of privacy. However, if the labyrinth is hidden away in a side room, although this may offer a comforting degree of privacy, the labyrinth itself can become vulnerable to damage and abuse, and the walkers may feel they are undertaking something furtive that they should be ashamed of. The ideal space would be one that is reasonably open and accessible, but also enables a feeling of intimacy and a degree of privacy for walkers. The room should have the potential to be locked at times when it is inconvenient for it to be closely monitored.

If the labyrinth is to be left available to walkers outside formal classroom hours, there should be a clear indication of where to seek help if the experience is at all distressing, either physically or mentally. Walking the labyrinth can cause extreme dizziness and feelings of nausea in some people. In others, the opportunity for calm and reflection may bring to the surface previously suppressed or unpleasant thoughts and feelings which a child or young person may be ill equipped to deal with at the time.

The other important factor is to ensure that the concept of the labyrinth has the support of the staff within the school. When considering the introduction of labyrinths by an outside agency – a church or education unit for example – the staff should be given an initial introduction to the history and possible uses of the labyrinth, and encouraged to voice concerns and ask questions at a very early stage. The opportunity should be given to staff to walk the labyrinth before using it in the classroom. Staff should be introduced to the concept of non-interference and non-intervention on the labyrinth, unless the walker is endangering themselves or others. It should be viewed by all as a safe place for reflection.

If possible, introduce the concept of the labyrinth, giving a brief history and some of the advantages of walking the labyrinth, to the whole school. If you are allowed to lead an assembly on the subject this can provide a short, focused amount of time to cover the basic historical, social and safety points. Use a slide or OHP of the pattern of labyrinth you are using to explain the concept of the single path, and ask the children for ways in which they think the labyrinth could be used – these answers are often most imaginative.

When working with the labyrinth in schools, large groups can be introduced to the pattern and its uses through the medium of talks and demonstrations. The etiquette of walking the labyrinth can be explained, as well as simple rules for its care and for the care of those walking it. However, after this introduction, the labyrinth is most effective when used in smaller groups – a maximum of 15 is best for producing a reflective environment conducive to discussion and exploration. It is important that enough time is allowed not only for students to experience the walk in whatever educational context it is presented, but to 'debrief' and reflect on the experience afterwards. There should also always be the reminder that if the experience is too distressing it can be ended at any time, and that there are staff members available for conversations and reassurance.

Potential uses

The labyrinth has the potential to be used in very many ways in a school environment, from simply enabling the children to experience the pattern, to the labyrinth becoming the focus of a number of activities in different academic areas, linking what might seem to be disparate subjects into a unified whole, giving children a holistic educational experience. However, all the suggestions listed below should be seen as secondary activities after the initial introduction to the labyrinth has taken place – the labyrinth will have much less impact if this primary step is omitted. Very often, there is only a limited time available for the children to experience the labyrinth – perhaps it has been brought into the school by a member of the church or has been borrowed for a single occasion. In this case, it is most useful if the children are divided into the size of group that can walk the labyrinth easily together.

This will be determined by the size of the labyrinth, but past experience has shown that 15 is a comfortable number – large enough for walkers not to feel isolated or self-conscious, but small enough to enable significant conversations to take place afterwards.

Outline for an introductory session to the labyrinth

This session should only take place after the initial preparatory work with staff or youth workers has been carried out. Make sure that you have set out all the equipment you think you might need, and that the site of the labyrinth is clear and ready for the children. Bring in the group and ask them to sit around the outside of the labyrinth, ideally just in front of the entrance, so that they can see the pattern easily. If you have enough copies, give the children a hand-held labyrinth pattern each so that they can trace the path first with their finger. This will help them to realize that there really is only one path, however confusing the pattern, and that they cannot get lost.

Introduce the group to the history of the labyrinth, emphasizing its universal nature and its appearance in many different cultures and continents, emphasizing the idea that to walk the labyrinth is to follow many other walkers through time and across countries. It is important that the simple rules of labyrinth walking are reinforced before a walk begins. It is helpful for those walking the labyrinth for the first time if it is undertaken in silence; this allows everyone an opportunity to experience it in their own individual way. Explain that since there is only one path into the centre and out again, it is inevitable that they will meet others going in a different direction, and that stepping aside for other walkers is a polite thing to do. Children should be encouraged to respect others walking on the labyrinth, allowing them space and silence in which to reflect and move.

Explain that there will be a time when a person will not be walking – they will either be waiting to start or waiting for others to finish – but that this time is also part of the labyrinth experience. Encourage those who are not actually walking to watch and wait in silence, reflecting on their own experiences. If the group appears very lively or is of an early primary age, then pens and paper can be offered, but the inevitable confusion and noise that will accompany the selection of pens and gathering of pieces of paper might prove offputting and disturbing to those still walking the labyrinth.

At the end of the walk, bring the group together to discuss how walking the labyrinth made them feel, and to think about the ways this activity made them view their own life journey. Simple open-ended questions can be asked such as 'How did this make you feel?', 'If your life is the path, where on the path do you think you are at the moment?', 'Which part of the path did you enjoy the most?', or 'What did it feel like to reach the centre/the outside again?'

Subject suggestion: PSHE (personal, social and health education)

For an open labyrinth walk such as this, keep the equipment to a minimum, providing only paper and pens and tissues. As the children become more familiar with the labyrinth, other ways to respond to the reflections and

thoughts it provokes, such as sand trays, modelling clay,
whiteboards, etc., can be introduced.

One of the most obvious uses of the labyrinth with
children and young people is simply to explore the effect
of the behaviour of individuals on others. As the children
walk into the labyrinth, they will of necessity meet others
walking out along the same path. This will necessitate
interaction and negotiation as the individuals try to walk
past each other without losing their own footing on the
path. Similarly, if walkers move at different speeds or in
different ways, the effect on other users of the labyrinth
will be noticeable. Questions can be asked after the walk
as to how it felt to be walking past others or negotiating
around them. This can lead on to explorations of how
our behaviour affects others, and from then, using the
language of metaphor, the way that our choices and
behaviour are influenced by those around us on our life
journey, and what impact our decision may have on those
of others.

The labyrinth can also be used to explore the concept
of the life journey and different stages in life. The metaphor of life as a journey can be used as a starting point
to examine different life stages, and the experiences and
emotions that might accompany them. Children can be
encouraged to consider where on their life journeys they
feel they have reached, and to look at the stages of those
around them. Suggestions for significant stages or achievements can be made, and rituals that are commonly used
to mark such stages explored, such as birthday parties,
weddings or partnership celebrations, memorial services,
etc. Labyrinths and mazes can be compared, with their
suitability as metaphors discussed – mazes offer choices,

wrong turnings and dead ends, whereas the path of the labyrinth is clearly defined and presents no detours or blind alleys.

Subject suggestion: Stress relief

The labyrinth has been used in many educational contexts as a way of helping children to control their levels of stress and anxiety, particularly during exam times. In this context the labyrinth should be introduced to a whole year group or class, with a brief discussion of its nature and possible purpose, and then laid out for pupils to use when they feel that they need to. It is particularly important when using the labyrinth as a stress buster to ensure that the site selected for it is itself quiet and calm-inducing – placing it in the hall of a busy school might only exacerbate feelings of anxiety and pressure. Find a place that is sufficiently far away from the general noise and confusion to give a feeling of seclusion, yet not so far that those walking it feel isolated or alone. If pupils are particularly sensitive to stress or if the events are felt to be highly stressful, then it is a good idea to maintain some low level of supervision for the labyrinth. This will not only prevent the labyrinth being used as a sports arena, but will also enable staff members to monitor the levels of distress of walkers so that they might be available for conversations afterwards.

Subject suggestion: Exploring creation

This exercise involves the construction of a labyrinth, so access to outside areas is necessary, as well as a supply of foliage, sticks, stones, etc., with which to build the labyrinth.

A very interesting way of enabling children and young people to engage with the labyrinth is to become involved in its creation. This could form part of an environment awareness programme, or curriculum enrichment, or be a unit of natural history study. Any green area will do in which to make a labyrinth – it could be the 'wilderness' area of a playground, a local nature reserve or even a park, although in the case of the latter it would be polite to clear the labyrinth away after its creation and use. Children could be introduced to the concept of the labyrinth in the classroom, and shown how to draw a classic three- or five-circuit labyrinth – these are easiest to construct in an outdoor setting. Once in the outdoors, sticks and other materials such as leaves or stones can be gathered, with older children being encouraged to look closely at the material they are collecting – first to assess its suitability for construction purposes, but also to focus on the object itself. Questions can be offered – what is this, does it come from a larger structure, how does it look? – that enable children to examine properly the natural debris that often goes unnoticed.

The entire group should be involved in the construction of the labyrinth – once the key points are fixed, filling in the walls can be done corporately. Children should be encouraged to create the walls as carefully as possible, paying attention to the material that is being used and the pattern of construction.

When the labyrinth has been built, encourage the group to walk it attentively. They should walk in silence, listening to the sounds of the environment around them. Questions can be offered to help with this listening – Can you hear any traffic, sounds of birds, any other creatures? Can you hear the sound of your own breathing, footsteps, the movements of others? Encourage stillness within the group to enable better attentiveness. A sense of alertness should also be fostered, with children encouraged to look at the environment surrounding them from the different perspectives that the labyrinth path gives.

Subject suggestion: Art and design

You will need as many different examples of labyrinth patterns as you can find, and the following:

> *Pens or crayons and paper.*
> *Shallow plastic trays filled with sand, sticks to draw with (chopsticks are ideal).*
> *Clay or playdough, tools for moulding.*
> *Paint, sponges, paper.*
> *Whiteboards and markers.*
> *For creating a full-scale labyrinth – several rolls of masking tape or sticks of chalk.*

One of the most obvious ways of enabling children and young people to grasp the concept of the labyrinth is to challenge them to create their own. Begin by showing different types of labyrinth – Wikimedia Commons has plenty of copyright-free examples which can be downloaded and photocopied. Try to include some black and white illustrations – younger children in particular will be able to get to grips with the idea of just one path following a curving and complicated route to a central point much more easily if they can follow the path with a pencil or crayon.

The next step is to move on to drawing a labyrinth to a pattern that already exists – the simplest of these being the classical three-circuit design. From this template, discussions can move into practising designs and experimenting with angles, curves, stopping places, etc. Participants should be reminded that designing a labyrinth can be difficult and challenging and may not in the end result in success. For this reason, pencil and paper might not be the best medium for these early explorations, as the amount of paper screwed up and thrown away as successive attempts are made at finding new and different labyrinth designs could soon become quite significant. Better tools might be small whiteboards, sand trays, pebbles or clay products. These will also have the advantage that the aspiring creator does not become too discouraged at so many failed attempts.

Once a labyrinth design has been arrived at by an individual, a group or a class, this can be drawn out on a larger scale. Masking tape or chalk are the best mediums for this stage, as mistakes can be easily removed, yet the finished product has some longevity. Alternatively the design can be painted on to paper or a low-cost fabric such as calico and used as a wall hanging.

Subject suggestion: Bible stories

You will need Bible stories, in an accessible format. Individual stories, particularly those with a journey theme, such as Joseph, Moses, the Nativity and the journey to Calvary, are especially appropriate.

A labyrinth can be used to bring to life many of the traditional Bible stories that involve journeying. Such stories abound in the Old Testament and in a fixed environment can lose much of their impact; such impact can be regained through travelling the labyrinth. In particular the story of the Exodus can be played out within the setting of the labyrinth in a way that enables children and young people to enter more fully into the concept of a transformative journey. It does not take 40 years to cross the Sinai Desert, however slowly people are moving, and the extra dimensions that transform a simple journey into a changing and formative experience can be explored within the circuitous paths of the labyrinth, crossing and re-crossing a small space focused on a central point. The development of the Israelites from a frightened bunch of runaway slaves into the Children of Israel is one of the focal points of the Old Testament, from which springs much of the understanding of what it means to be a child of God, and as such deserves to be imbued with the drama that the labyrinth can provide. Other journeys include that of Ruth and Naomi, Elijah and Elisha, Jacob, Joseph.

The labyrinth can also be used to consider the idea of liminal experiences – times of growth and transformation that take place outside of the usual environment of civilization. In this context, Jesus' stay in the wilderness and his frequent withdrawals to pray can be brought to life via the labyrinth. Other journeys, such as those made by Mary and Joseph in the early years of Christ's life, from Nazareth to Bethlehem, and then to Egypt before returning to Nazareth, can also be highlighted, with understanding shared of the perilous situation for the Holy Family at this time. Such experiences, played out on the labyrinth, can in turn lead to a better understanding of today's wandering people – refugees, displaced people, and runaways. The Easter story, from the triumphal entry into Jerusalem, along the paths to the Mount of Olives, the courts and that final hill of Calvary, can also be told as a journey, with stops – similar to those of the Stations of the Cross – included along the way.

In these contexts the labyrinth can be used as a backdrop for the story, with children encouraged to hear the story before walking the labyrinth, or as the story itself, with different parts of the story shared during the walk itself. If no full-size labyrinth is available, hand-held labyrinths can be used, although much of the corporate nature of biblical journeys is lost.

Subject suggestion: Pilgrimage

The concept of pilgrimage is explored in both primary and secondary schools, at Key Stage 2 and for GCSE Religious Studies. The labyrinth as a substitute for pilgrimage, and as a way of sharing the pilgrimage experience without leaving the school environment, can be an invaluable teaching aid. Students should first be introduced to the concept of pilgrimage as a spiritual journey to a sacred place, with a significant role in the major religions. Additional reasons for travel can also be explored – those seeking healing both physical and mental; pilgrims looking for a challenge and adventure; or the desire to experience some time that is free from the everyday restraints of contemporary life. Key Christian pilgrimage sites can be mentioned, with their origins dating back to medieval times. The possible use of labyrinth as a substitute for these pilgrim places during times of conflict and unrest, when the risks of travelling across countries and continents, already high, were increased to a level that made pilgrimage impossible, should be used as a way of introducing the labyrinth. Labyrinths were found in churches and cathedrals across Europe, and walking them can be a way of connecting with the past in a form that engages the whole being, not just the intellect. A mini-pilgrimage can be walked out, with students considering the items that they might take with them, and comparing them with the equipment of a medieval pilgrim. The journey's destination, at the centre of the labyrinth, can be discussed, with an exploration of the different rituals that might take place at various shrines – for example, kissing the statue of St James behind the altar at Santiago de Compostela, or participating in Mass at St Peter's Square in Rome. Small souvenirs, such as shells and keys, can be collected at the centre as a reminder of the souvenirs that pilgrims collected on their travels. With the labyrinth, the journey back from the shrine, often neglected by historians, but by no means free from dangers, can also regain some significance, with a final discussion of the difficulties of returning home after a long time away, leading into a consideration of the effects of change and growth on self and others.

Subject Suggestion: Music

You will need examples of 'journeying music' from as many different traditions and as many different styles as possible, and musical instruments for individual experimentation and exploration.

Any group of people that walks any distance soon produces music to help the journey along, whether they are soldiers advancing to battle, protest marchers, pilgrims or religious processions. After enabling children to engage with the concept of the labyrinth, through information, discussion and an experience of the labyrinth itself, it can be interesting and challenging to consider the types of music that best enable interaction with the labyrinth. There are CDs available of the sort of music that medieval pilgrims might have expected to hear on their journeys, from Spanish tavern songs, to chants sung while walking the road, as well as those used in cathedrals and churches along the way.

Military music, popular songs and classical music that takes journeying as its inspiration can be explored as the discussion broadens. Students can be encouraged to consider the type of music that they might find helpful for their own journey on the labyrinth, as well as the effect that different tempos and styles of music might have on their speed and the nature of their reflections. Compositions of music specifically for the labyrinth can be explored, with students given the opportunity to try out their own compositions and those of other class members.

Worship event
BEGINNING THE SCHOOL YEAR

The beginning of the school year can be a very effective time for introducing students to the labyrinth. An opportunity to walk the labyrinth together can encourage community thinking, and the skills needed to negotiate around each other as they journey to and from the centre can promote courtesy and awareness of others. It can also teach students the benefits of labyrinth walking to ease stress and encourage concentration, so that if the labyrinth is available at other times, they will be equipped to benefit from what it can offer.

OPENING

This is the day the Lord has made
Let us rejoice and be glad in it.

Heavenly Father, we thank you that we can be gathered here today to celebrate the beginning of another year. Help us to focus on our studies and to work together for the good of this school community. Help us to be aware of your presence with us as we journey on, leading us along right pathways and supporting us in times of difficulty.

SUGGESTED READINGS

The LORD was with Samuel as he grew up, and he let none of Samuel's words fall to the ground. And all Israel from Dan to Beersheba recognised that Samuel was attested as a prophet of the LORD. The LORD

continued to appear at Shiloh, and there he revealed
himself to Samuel through his word.
1 Samuel 3.19–21 (NIV)

I will extol the LORD with all my heart
in the council of the upright and in the assembly.

Great are the works of the LORD;
they are pondered by all who delight in them.
Glorious and majestic are his deeds,
and his righteousness endures for ever.
He has caused his wonders to be remembered;
the LORD is gracious and compassionate.
He provides food for those who fear him;
he remembers his covenant for ever.
He has shown his people the power of his works,
giving them the lands of other nations.
The works of his hands are faithful and just;
all his precepts are trustworthy.
They are established for ever and ever,
enacted in faithfulness and uprightness.
He provided redemption for his people;
he ordained his covenant for ever –
holy and awesome is his name.

The fear of the LORD is the beginning of wisdom;
all who follow his precepts have good understanding.
To him belongs eternal praise.
Psalm 111 (NIV)

Every year Jesus' parents went to Jerusalem for the Festival of the Passover. When he was twelve years old, they went up to the festival, according to the custom. After the festival was over, while his parents were returning home, the boy Jesus stayed behind in Jerusalem, but they were unaware of it. Thinking he was in their company, they travelled on for a day. Then they began looking for him among their relatives and friends. When they did not find him, they went back to Jerusalem to look for him. After three days they found him in the temple courts, sitting among the teachers, listening to them and asking them questions. Everyone who heard him was amazed at his understanding and his answers. When his parents saw him, they were astonished. His mother said to him, 'Son, why have you treated us like this? Your father and I have been anxiously searching for you.'

'Why were you searching for me?' he asked. 'Didn't you know I had to be in my Father's house?' But they did not understand what he was saying to them.

Then he went down to Nazareth with them and was obedient to them. But his mother treasured all these things in her heart. And Jesus grew in wisdom and stature, and in favour with God and man.
Luke 2.41–52 (NIV)

LABYRINTH ACTIVITY

Provide pencils and paper.

Ask the children to draw around their feet, either with shoes and socks on or barefoot, as is most appropriate. If there is time, children can decorate their feet, or this could be done as a preparatory activity before the service. Once this has been done, cut out the feet shapes.

Fasten the feet shapes to the paths of the labyrinth. If the labyrinth is made from masking tape or drawn in chalk, the feet can form the pattern of the labyrinth itself. If a canvas or permanent labyrinth is being used, the feet can be attached to the labyrinth with Blu-Tack or masking tape.

If the feet have been previously coloured in and cut out, they can be stuck on to the labyrinth before the beginning of the service. This is preferable as it obviates the necessity for careful monitoring. However, if the group is sufficiently small in number, the students can walk on to the labyrinth holding their feet shapes and whatever is necessary to fasten them to the labyrinth. Then, when they reach somewhere they feel is appropriate, they can put the paper foot in place.

As the students walk, encourage them to consider the challenges and adventures that are waiting for them during the school year, and to ask God for the wisdom to make right choices. Remind them that walking the labyrinth does not require choices, but it does need concentration if the path is to be followed.

At the end of the walk, invite the students to look at the pattern of the feet on the labyrinth. They will be in different places and look as if the footprints are headed in different directions. But they are all headed in the same way, just as all the students and staff are part of one community, even if it does not look that way at times!

PRAYERS

Father of all, help us to be mindful of the wonders that surround us as we begin this school year – of opportunities for learning, for friendship and for fun. Help us to journey reflectively, taking time to consider our surroundings and those who share them, and help us to rejoice in them all.

> The Almighty and everlasting God, Who is the Way, the Truth, and the Life, dispose your journey according to His good pleasure; send his angel Raphael to keep you in this your pilgrimage, and both conduct you in peace on your way to the place where you would be, and bring you back again on your return to us in safety.
>
> *Sarum Missal 1150*

Help us, Lord, in all that we say and do, with all whom we meet and everything we see, to seek your will and respond to your love. **Amen**

CLOSING

May God bless you as you begin your journey
Let us follow the Lord's path with a faithful heart and in loving service.

Worship event
SCHOOL LEAVERS' SERVICE

A labyrinth walk can be a very powerful symbol of journeying on, containing both a journey into the centre and
travel outwards again. To some, this might seem as if
one's steps are being retraced, but the emphasis should be
upon the things the children have learnt during their time
at the school, and the things they want to take with them
as they move on. In this way, the inward journey can be a
process of recollection and celebration, and the outward
journey one of anticipation and adventure.

OPENING

Invite three leavers to approach and light the candles.
These can be either in the centre of the labyrinth or on an
altar if the service takes place in a church. Large electric
candles may be considered a safer option than real ones.

Light candle one

'Lay down what is past and look to the future.'

Light candle two

'Care for each other as you remember God's love for you.'

Light candle three

'Journey on in peace.'
Heavenly Father, as we reach the end of our time in this
school, we thank you for the time we have spent here.
We remember celebrations and achievements, activities
and learning, all taking place in the company of our fel-

low journey companions. As we mark this time, make us grateful for all that we have received, and able to look forward to a continued time of learning and companionship. Be our guide as we journey onwards, and give us the grace to see your signs and follow your path.'

SUGGESTED READINGS

By day the LORD went ahead of them in a pillar of cloud to guide them on their way and by night in a pillar of fire to give them light, so that they could travel by day or night. Neither the pillar of cloud by day nor the pillar of fire by night left its place in front of the people.
Exodus 13.21–22 (NIV)

Show me your ways, LORD, teach me your paths.
Guide me in your truth and teach me,
for you are God my Saviour,
and my hope is in you all day long.
Remember, LORD, your great mercy and love,
for they are from of old.
Do not remember the sins of my youth
and my rebellious ways;
according to your love remember me,
for you, LORD, are good.

Good and upright is the LORD;
therefore he instructs sinners in his ways.
He guides the humble in what is right
and teaches them his way.
All the ways of the LORD are loving and faithful
towards those who keep the demands of his covenant.
Psalm 25.4–10 (NIV)

Let the peace of Christ rule in your hearts, since as members of one body you were called to peace. And be thankful. Let the message of Christ dwell among you richly as you teach and admonish one another with all wisdom through psalms, hymns, and songs from the Spirit, singing to God with gratitude in your hearts. And whatever you do, whether in word or deed, do it all in the name of the Lord Jesus, giving thanks to God the Father through him.
Colossians 3.15–17 (NIV)

LABYRINTH ACTIVITY

As a preparatory activity, ask the students who are leaving to decorate garden stones in whatever colours or patterns they like. The best stones for this purpose are the large garden cobbles that can be purchased at any garden centre. You will need to wash and dry them first, however. Allow two stones per leaver, but only one is to be painted.

In the centre of the labyrinth, make a cairn with the unpainted stones. Ask the students to take their decorated stone into the centre of the labyrinth and leave it there. This is a sign both of all the things they have learnt and the way they have grown during their time at the school and also of the impact they have made on the community in their turn. If the walk can be preceded by some times of remembering, with other children speaking about the leavers, this will be even more powerful.

When each stone has been placed in the centre, the student should then pick up an unpainted stone and carry it out. This is a sign of hope and looking forward, as the plain stone will be carried on into the future, to

be decorated in its turn with all that is to be learnt or
achieved during the next stage of life.

PRAYERS

Lord God, we thank you for the time we have spent at
this school. We pray for those who are leaving now,
and for those who will stay behind. We pray for communities new and old, for friendships that have yet
to be made, and for friends who journey with us. We
pray that we may be aware of your love guarding us,
and that we listen to the words of guidance that you
whisper to our hearts. **Amen**

Disturb us, Lord, when we are too well pleased with
  ourselves,
When our dreams have come true
Because we have dreamed too little,
When we arrived safely
Because we sailed too close to the shore.

Disturb us, Lord, when
With the abundance of things we possess
We have lost our thirst
For the waters of life;
Having fallen in love with life
We have ceased to dream of eternity,
And in our efforts to build a new earth
We have allowed our vision
Of the new heaven to dim.

Disturb us, Lord, to dare more boldly,
To venture on wider seas,
Where storms will show your mastery,
Where losing sight of land
We shall find the stars.

We ask you to push back
The horizons of our hopes
And to push into the future
in strength, courage, hope and love.
Sir Francis Drake, c. 1540–1596

CLOSING

May the Lord watch over your coming and your going
both now and evermore
**Let us journey onwards, rejoicing in God and grateful for
the company of others.**

6

Using Labyrinths in Different Contexts

Introduction

Labyrinth walks can take place in many different contexts and settings, although the basic issues such as providing a safe, quiet space for walkers, with somewhere to reflect afterwards, as well as considerations of publicity, planning and relevance, are universal. However, there are some considerations that are particularly appropriate when using the labyrinth within specific contexts, and this chapter explores the use of labyrinths in some widely differing settings. Experienced leaders working with the labyrinth within these contexts were visited and interviewed, and although the experiences are all personal, the lessons that can be drawn from them are easy to apply more widely.

Mental health care

The use of labyrinths within a mental health care context has not so far been very widespread. There is evidence that some practitioners have used labyrinths as a means of coping with the stress of the working environment, but few instances of their use among those suffering from mental health problems. However, this number is growing as the capacity of the labyrinth to encourage mindfulness and reflection in a way that assists walkers to focus and calm themselves is becoming more widely known.

One person who has worked in this area is Harry Smart, who has worked as an NHS Chaplain, specializing in the area of mental health in Lincolnshire. He was among the first to use the labyrinth to enable both inpatients and those living in the community to explore issues of spirituality.

The first group he worked with was one that he had been facilitating in partnership with a drama therapist. As one set of sessions came to an end, they decided that the labyrinth might be a useful way in for exploring themes of journey and moving on. As well as members of the previous drama group, others were also attracted to the group because of the labyrinth.

Harry was careful to clear his programme with his manager, and to include a clear schedule and a system of feedback in line with NHS Chaplaincy requirements. As already stated, this is a very important part of preparing the way for labyrinth workshops in such a context. His plan was for seven sessions, including a final one for feedback. Harry felt that the metaphor of the labyrinth could help individuals engage with their spirituality and search for meaning, as well as developing ways of engaging with the changes that were occurring in their lives – such as change in patient status, relationships and living space.

The make-up of the group eventually consisted of former hospital inpatients who had made the transition to outpatient status. They were engaged in the challenge of living with bipolar disorder, anxiety, depression and

similar conditions, and were facing the issues and difficulties that this involved. The group was self-selected;
some were members of the drama group that had previously been running; others came in response to the notices
sent out across the Trust, via service user groups and
community psychiatric nurses. Harry's initial aim was for
the group to be inclusive, but also to be committed to the
entire journey of all seven sessions. In the end this was
difficult to achieve, but there were enough members of
the group who came to all the sessions to give the group a
coherence and sense of continuity and community.

The course followed the broad theme of pilgrimage,
and the concept of the labyrinth was introduced from
the beginning with the use of finger labyrinths in the first
session. This was so that although there was an element
of anticipation in the idea that the penultimate session
would consist of walking a labyrinth, this was a manage-
able challenge and not a potentially threatening event in
the future. The finger labyrinths were given to the group
members for use both in the first session and for home
use thereafter, and many reported that this helped them
to centre and focus.

The sessions lasted about an hour and included discussions on the nature of pilgrimage and different types
of pilgrimage, who the group members took on their
journey, things that were left behind. Harry made use
of pictures, quotes about pilgrimage, images of different
characters, and two of the sessions included elements
of drama. They explored the tension between 'where I
am at the moment' and 'where I would like to be' and
examined ways of dealing with the gap between ideal
and actual. Sessions began with an electric candle being
passed around as members shared their feelings or some

aspect of the day they had experienced, and ended with a simple circle dance that symbolized the coming together and moving apart of the group's formation, interaction and departure.

For the penultimate session, the meeting room was divided in two using a folding partition, and individuals were invited to walk the labyrinth – either alone or accompanied by Harry. Most chose to walk alone, returning to the group after their walk to share their experiences. It was felt that the usual procedure of witnessing the walk of others before walking it oneself was too threatening for the group; the emphasis at all times was on enabling individuals to explore their spirituality in a safe environment. People walked the labyrinth at different speeds and had differing experiences, but all used the labyrinth as a metaphor for their own life journeys and challenges.

The labyrinth was also used as the core object for an inpatient group in the rehabilitation centre, but in this context it proved more equivocal in its success at enabling spiritual conversations to take place. Many of those attending found the metaphor of journey a useful source of vocabulary with which to describe their spirituality, but the coherence of the group suffered from lack of regular attendance by some members. Active support from the wards for the group, ideally with members of staff attending, is a very helpful factor here. Also beneficial would be to spend some time working with a group before introducing the labyrinth, and then to offer some sort of follow-up after the course, rather than 'parachute' such a powerful tool into such a context. As with all facilitators of labyrinth groups and workshops, careful and sensitive leadership is vitally important, as well as a readiness to engage with the various issues that may develop as the group progresses, influenced either by events within the group or those occurring in the wider community.

End of life care – Maggie's Centre, Dundee

The labyrinth outside Maggie's Centre in Dundee was designed to integrate the centre with its surrounding landscape and provide a continuation to the pathway linking the Centre to the main hospital site. Set within a series of raised banks that form an amphitheatre for the design, the labyrinth is immediately outside the front door of the Centre, reflecting the gentle curves of the building and its wavy roof. The harmony of the building with the landscape is echoed by the peaceful welcome of the interior space, divided into comfortable spaces, with a focal kitchen area providing physical, mental and psychological refreshment. The purpose of the Centre is to give psychological and emotional support for those living with cancer, through a variety of resources and approaches, with a concern for holistic wellbeing.

With a focus on relaxation and stress management, the labyrinth has a significant part to play in providing an outside landscape suitable for exploration and meditation. A relaxation therapist has used the labyrinth as part of a four-week meditation course, and it has been a useful resource for creative writing and art therapists, who have held events on the labyrinth as a source of inspiration and connectivity. There are plans to widen the invitation to walk the labyrinth to the staff, patients and visitors of the main hospital site, which is at present slightly detached from the labyrinth. Information on the benefits of labyrinth walking for stress reduction, team building and conflict management will shortly be available and it is hoped that some of the main departments will make use of this beautiful resource.

As with all institutions with a constantly changing user group, there is significant effort involved in maintaining awareness of the potential of the labyrinth. In such a demanding environment as cancer support, emotional and physical resources can easily be over-stretched, making it important that the time involved in planning and presenting labyrinth events should be carefully factored into work schedules.

Schools – The Coombes CE Primary School, Arborfield

The logo of The Coombes School is, as the children were able to affirm, the Chartres labyrinth, and the school remains loyal to its logo in its imaginative and creative use of different types of labyrinth for many areas of the curriculum. Originally the initiative of the infant school head teacher, who had been using labyrinths within the school since 2006, the two-coloured design was adopted when the school combined with a junior school in 2008, and has remained a vital and relevant part of the ethos of the school ever since.

The school has a semi-permanent labyrinth, taken from a Native American design made from a base of woodchips, with the paths outlined with bits of broken paving. It sits at the edge of a playing field, sloping gently down to a less cultivated area of playground, giving a variety of vistas to look out upon during a walk. The labyrinth is refurbished regularly, with the head teacher himself barrowing over the woodchips necessary to renew the base, and other members of staff helping to tidy up the stone outline. This labyrinth is an integral part of the school grounds, forming an organic part of the landscape of winding paths, wild areas and wooden play structures, which together with the traditional asphalt make up the play areas. Children are able to walk this when they feel the need for some reflective time. Occasionally children may be encouraged to do this by a member of staff, but usually a walk is child initiated.

However, the heart of the school's labyrinth work does not lie here, but with a full-size replica of the Chartres labyrinth. Towards the end of the summer holidays, when the weather is set fair for the two or three days necessary for the paint to dry, the former head teacher and staff of the school paint the labyrinth design in white emulsion on the school playing field. Then, as part of the school's celebration of the commencement of the new school year, the entire 600-strong school, pupils and staff alike, walk the labyrinth. They do this all together, observing very carefully the protocols of enabling reflection by being assiduous at avoiding bumping into each other along the path, not overtaking each other, and respecting the musicians who are playing in the central rose of the labyrinth during the walk by keeping silent throughout the event. It is a rite of beginning, a celebration of community, a welcoming and drawing in of new members to the school, and a time-honoured ritual from the school's corporate history. It is also, as many of the children affirm, a time to remember those who are not able to walk the labyrinth, absent through illness, relocation or even death.

The painted walls of the labyrinth soon fade in this country's wet climate, but instead the paths become highlighted as the children's feet wear down the grass as they make the journey. The labyrinth continues to be used to enrich many parts of the school curriculum – dances are choreographed within its space; music is made upon it and about it; the history of the labyrinth design and its various uses within different cultures is explored. Eventually, as the winter draws on, the labyrinth design fades completely, to await resurrection the following year. This is encouraged by the head, who prefers the temporary nature of the emulsion as it concentrates labyrinth work to within a short teaching period. It also enables flexibility of timetabling and lesson planning and ensures that the school is not burdened with a resource for which it no longer has a particular use.

Further education – The University of Edinburgh

The arrival of the outdoor labyrinth in George Square, Edinburgh, was very much due to the chaplaincy department. New to the University Chaplaincy, Di Williams was already aware of the value of labyrinths as a way of enabling 'embodied prayer', and of holding and developing dialogue within a safe place. With the help of a training grant, she travelled to San Francisco to train as a labyrinth facilitator with Lauren Artress, discovering on her return to Edinburgh that her active campaigning and petitioning for funding a canvas labyrinth had at last paid off.

The canvas labyrinth was used a great deal in the following years – it was initially laid out once a week in a space within the chaplaincy, which became once a month after a year. This was because the community had become sufficiently aware of the labyrinth to allow the intensity of the introduction to lessen and also because the level of demands upon the small chaplaincy staff were too great to sustain. As well as a regular event, the labyrinth was also set up during Freshers' Week, at exam times, and during wellbeing awareness events. These last were particularly important in convincing the funding authorities, both internal and external, that the construction of an outdoor labyrinth would provide a useful resource for enabling and promoting wellbeing among the students and staff of the institution. Another successful grant application, made after years of careful and dedicated demonstrations of the value of the labyrinth as a tool for the promotion of spiritual and holistic wellbeing, meant that Di's vision of an outdoor labyrinth could finally be realized. This was achieved with the help of a university architect who was already familiar with the concept of the labyrinth, and with a local construction team.

Today the labyrinth is managed by an external labyrinth chaplain, a rector of an Edinburgh church, who liaises with the University Chaplaincy to promote the use of the labyrinth in a variety of ways. Walks are facilitated at regular intervals on both the outdoor and canvas labyrinths, with a particular emphasis continuing to be placed on its use during Freshers' Week, at exam time, and as part of university-wide initiatives promoting wellbeing. Several smaller canvas labyrinths have been made with the help of students and these are used within smaller areas such as the chaplaincy offices, and the communal areas of student halls of residence, providing a range of resources for enabling spiritual exploration and encounter. The current labyrinth chaplain, Frances Burberry, also finds the outdoor labyrinth useful for conversations with those students who would be reluctant to engage with a chaplain – or indeed enter the chaplaincy building at all. The openness of the space, set within one of the garden squares of the city, encourages a corresponding openness of dialogue, while the feel of safety generated by the labyrinth itself promotes confidence. Di Williams has also used the labyrinth for group counselling events run in partnership with student counselling services. After a brief introduction to the labyrinth, groups of students are invited to walk the labyrinth. Following a period of time during which the students were encouraged to respond to their walk, the group was reconvened by a counsellor, and the students invited to unpack their experiences. This was felt to be a very successful example of partnership within the services of the University.

The chaplains stressed the importance of the labyrinth being 'owned' by the institution, and by the student body, although the difficulties of ensuring a continuity of support due to the fleeting nature of the student population should not be underestimated. Constant work is demanded of the chaplains to ensure that awareness of the labyrinth and its potential remains at a good level. Careful use of appropriate language that can be understood by interested parties and that relates to the current concerns of the governing body and other groups is vital to maintain the good standing of the labyrinth within the community. In a broader context, the amount of time needed to initiate, develop, promote and maintain labyrinth spirituality within an institution should not be ignored.

Careful consideration must be given to the amount of time available and the effect this will have on other resources offered by the chaplaincy. By engaging an external facilitator to undertake the management of the labyrinth, the chaplaincy has been enabled to continue a wide range of other services and resources, and offers a useful example.

Frances also negotiates with external organizations for the use of the outdoor labyrinth which, although built on University grounds, is in a space that is open to the public during daylight hours. She ensures the material safety of the labyrinth and monitors the use to which it is put by other organizations in a way that encourages a good relationship between the city and the University.

Cathedrals – Norwich Cathedral

The labyrinth at Norwich Cathedral inhabits its space as if it had been installed at the same time as the building of the cloisters that encircle it. In fact, the cathedral architect made adjustments to the original design for the labyrinth so that it would resonate with the sacred geometry of the cathedral, and the resulting widening of the pathway reflects the patterns and angles of the cloisters themselves. The extra space at the turns, demonstrated by the worn path of so many walkers, becomes a pausing place for those who wish to reflect out of the way of other walkers, and offers potential for prayer stations along the way.

Installed in 2002, the labyrinth at the cathedral offers both the casual visitor and the more intentional walker the opportunity to reflect and pray in harmonious surroundings. Both Gudrun Warren, the Librarian, and Peter Doll, the Canon Librarian, report that the labyrinth is well used, particularly by the casual visitor or tourist. This is interesting, as many labyrinths in other public locations are not used in this way. Perhaps this reflects the nature of the cathedral visitor – already curious about their environment, they are more prepared to take a risk on something previously untried. The free guide to the cathedral offers suggestions for walking the labyrinth, inviting visitors to use it as a space to pause and reflect.

The labyrinth is also used by the cathedral in a more intentional way, although due to the large number of services and events being held there, this use – although regular – is not frequent. Four times a year Norwich Cathedral offers 'Silence in the Cathedral' – an opportunity to experience the entire building in silence, exploring both interior and exterior space and prayer. Weather permitting, the labyrinth is available for participants and is 'dressed' for the occasion. This usually involves highlighting the stones which mark the pathway in ways that reflect the theme of the event. Thus for Advent, each stone was topped with a lit candle, which in the darkness of the evening gave the labyrinth a significant aspect of 'otherness'. For Corpus Christi, the stones were sprinkled with rose petals. These additions are reported as having a signal effect on the feel and aspect of the walk, something commented on by cathedral staff and visitors alike.

The situation of the labyrinth has its challenges – those unfamiliar with its use can disregard it or disturb intentional walkers, or indeed it can be 'kidnapped' by those who wish to use it for purposes other than the one for which it is intended. Its situation in the cloisters is very open, which is inviting for the casual visitor, but, surrounded as it is by windows, can present a public aspect that is too threatening for the walker who wishes to reflect in private. Popularity increases environmental vulnerability, and in poor weather or after a busy season, the labyrinth must be closed to allow for recovery and repair. However, despite these difficulties, there is no doubt in the minds of users and caretakers of the labyrinth that it offers a valuable opportunity for prayer and reflection in addition to, and in harmony with, those opportunities offered by the rest of the sacred space within the cathedral.

Churches – St Michael and All Angels, Abingdon

St Michael and All Angels Church has an enviable situation set within the middle of a beautifully landscaped Victorian park in the centre of Abingdon, surrounded by a crescent of large family homes, adjacent to Abingdon School, an independent boys' school. On arriving at St Michael's, the vicar accompanied the church community in their discernment exercise regarding the particular gifts that the church community could offer the wider community within the town. Anglo-Catholic in worship style, the church is a favourite location for weddings during the summer months, but did not interact with the civic community in any other particular way. The church community sought to address this by creating a meaningful space for community events and meetings. The church council and congregation engaged in a long period of preparatory exploration and discernment before the final plans for the removal of the pews and the creation of a vibrant distinctive space could be approved. A 'pilgrim liturgy' was used for several years beforehand to prepare the ground for the congregation to perceive the desirability of a flexible and open liturgical space.

In close parallel with the desire to create a space was the objective of liberating the spirit of that space, and early in the discussion it was felt that a labyrinth design could be used to articulate the already implicit pilgrim identity of the people of God in a more explicit way. A specialist team of labyrinth designers and builders were invited to join the discussions and a plan was reached that fulfilled the requirements of church building, community and labyrinth alike. By great good fortune, a pattern of a labyrinth was discovered in an eleventh-century manuscript of a book produced by the former Abbey at Abingdon, and it was this six-path, seven-wall design, unique to Abingdon, that was used, giving the building a link with the past not only of the church, but of the entire community.

For the congregation of St Michael's, the labyrinth embodies the pilgrim identity of the people of God. It enables a more open relationship with the concept of a spiritual journey than that which it is possible to enter into from a stationary position within a fixed pew. Liturgies have been designed which travel around the church, using the labyrinth as the location for the Liturgy of the Word, but remaining true to St Michael's tradition of worship by celebrating the Eucharist within the chancel. This liturgy 'enacts the reality of God's pilgrim people by moving them on the journey of the Christian life from baptism through this world to the eschatological banquet of the kingdom'.

Use of the labyrinth by groups and individuals has remained active, as fortunately the succeeding incumbent is also enthusiastic about labyrinth spirituality. There is a regular monthly labyrinth event: 'Silent Reflections', which is facilitated by a number of lay members of the church community. This event begins with a meditation in the church room, followed by an opportunity to walk the labyrinth or simply reflect in the silence of the church. A number of Quiet Days are also hosted by St Michael's and the labyrinth is regularly used by other organizations within the town and further afield. The workload of facilitation and organization is managed by an enthusiastic lay member of the church, who has also ensured succession by gathering a group of enthusiasts to share the events. It is hoped that the labyrinth will be made more generally accessible but, as is often the case, the church community is challenged by the logistical difficulties of keeping the church open for casual and interested walkers other than those who arrive for organized events.

Retreat centres – The Society of Mary and Martha

The Society of Mary and Martha at Sheldon in Devon was founded in 1991 by Carl Lee, concerned at the effect of stress and overwork on clergy. Today it is a thriving community, with an effective and loving ministry aimed particularly at providing a place of rest and recuperation for ministers of the Church.

The advantages of providing a labyrinth as part of the resources offered to those staying at Sheldon had long been apparent to the members of its community. However, the technical problems of finding a suitable site seemed overwhelming. The community is situated on the side of a hill, with wonderful views over the surrounding countryside, but offering few spaces flat enough to house a labyrinth, and those few being needed as car parks and access points. Experiments with a 'prayer meadow' – a wandering path mown into a hillside meadow over the course of a summer – had established the desirability of an open prayer space, but also highlighted the issues attached to it.

The cost of constructing a labyrinth from stone is considerable, and the community felt that such a significant outlay of capital would be better spent improving current facilities. Other types of labyrinth brought with them the question of ongoing maintenance, and this too threatened to be a drain on already tight resources – the prayer meadow, while undoubtedly proving itself as a useful spiritual resource, had taken up much time in its mowing and care.

The opportunity to change this situation arose as a consequence of building developments on the site. Initial ideas to incorporate a small labyrinth into the paved area outside a new meeting room were not taken up as it was felt that installing a small labyrinth, overlooked by users of the building, would be prohibitively expensive and not provide a sufficiently private place for reflective prayer.

Instead, imaginative use was made of an area further to the north of the building that had been levelled as part of the re-landscaping to dispose of excavated material from the construction works. It soon appeared that the area of the space would just fit a full-size Chartres-style labyrinth. The community team, with the help of volunteers, set out to design and build a labyrinth themselves. A weed-suppressing membrane was first laid down, followed by crushed road stone as a base. The pattern was marked out first with a white line machine, then in small basalt blocks as the outline of the path, the rest being filled in with self-compacting path gravel. The resulting labyrinth faces west across the Devon hills, its entrance guarded by two upright granite stones that allow walkers into the labyrinth area. Embraced by trees, the site offers a private reflective space which is beautifully in tune with its surroundings.

Perhaps due to the nature of its development and construction, emerging as it did from the heart of the community and its desire to offer peace and space to those who most need it, the labyrinth forms a balanced, organic whole with the site and this is echoed in the way it is used. The programme for the Society of Mary and Martha at Sheldon offers labyrinth retreats and 'taster days', but the labyrinth is not so much a structured prayer discipline as an overall offering of the community to its resident guests. Occasionally a labyrinth walk will be suggested to individuals seeking time to reflect or space in which to make difficult decisions, but most walkers simply find themselves there and make their own personal walk of discovery. It is a particular gift to those who feel disconnected from their regular prayer life, due to stress or illness, offering an embodied experience of simplicity and peace within a secure space.

Conclusion

One of the wonderful features about labyrinths is that every visit to a labyrinth site indicates the way to further sites. Conversations with owners or keepers of one labyrinth will bring introductions to others, and gradually a picture emerges of a network of enthusiastic labyrinth walkers throughout the country. Labyrinths have been built in many different situations and used in a huge variety of contexts. Initially some of these contexts can seem hostile to the concept of a labyrinth – a busy city centre, for example, with a large amount of traffic rushing past, or a small, L-shaped urban back garden. However, with careful planning and a sensitive choice of labyrinth pattern and activity, even the most challenging spaces can be overcome.

7

Labyrinth Resources and Further Reading

Labyrinths

One of the problems of locating labyrinths within the UK is that there is still no exhaustive gazetteer of where they can be found. The best tool to use is the Labyrinth Locator, which is jointly run by Veriditas and the Labyrinth Society. This has a list of indoor and outdoor labyrinths, but by no means does it contain all the labyrinths that have been built. During the course of research for this book the author discovered many more labyrinth builders and designers, and some of the wide range of labyrinths that had been created, but it was a difficult exercise. Perhaps the best way to find a labyrinth near your location is to begin with the ones listed in the Locator and then enquire of the owners/organizers as to whether they know of any more in the area. Very often these people will be aware of other enthusiasts within their area and can help you get in touch with them. Creators of labyrinths, both indoors and outdoors, may be found not only in the context of labyrinth designers, such as the Labyrinth Builders, but architects and garden designers also have put their hand to the design and installation of labyrinths within buildings and landscapes. Looking at their websites can help to identify recent labyrinth projects that may be available to use.

Many retreat centres have now installed either inside or, more commonly, outside labyrinths to help promote a meditative and reflective atmosphere. Some churches and cathedrals too have installed labyrinths either in their churchyards, or less usually within the church building. Here, too, persistence is required in order to locate nearby labyrinths.

Events

If you are looking for a labyrinth event in which to participate, the Retreat Association is a good place to start, but there are several freelance labyrinth facilitators within the UK who offer workshops and lectures either at a venue of your own choosing or elsewhere. If you are seeking a specifically Christian labyrinth leader, it is safest still to look for 'Veriditas-trained' leaders. These have been trained by Lauren Artress, who spearheaded the Christian labyrinth revival in the 1980s; she was originally from Grace Cathedral, where she was Dean, and now operates independently through the auspices of the labyrinth organization Veriditas. The UK has only one Master Trainer, Di Williams, who is able to deliver labyrinth facilitator training (www.diwilliams.com). These two-day workshops are expensive, but it is worth gathering together a group of people to fund a labyrinth facilitator training event. The Diocese of Lincoln recently organized such an event as part of its Spirituality programme of engagement with the labyrinth which was

RESOURCES AND FURTHER READING

rolled out across the Diocese. This involved churches, retreat centres, schools, community groups and Lincoln Cathedral itself in a programme of workshops, events and demonstrations, as well as the opportunity to walk the newly purchased canvas labyrinths. Alternatively, trips can be made to Chartres, France or various locations in the USA to obtain facilitator training, as well as training in building temporary and permanent labyrinths through www.veriditas.org.

Creating your own

If you wish to lead your own labyrinth event in your own location, your best option will be either to borrow a canvas labyrinth or to lay out your own labyrinth. Canvas labyrinths can be difficult to obtain, but a good place to start could be your local diocesan office or resource centre, which may be able to put you in touch with owners of canvas labyrinths, if they do not possess one of their own.

Otherwise, labyrinths can easily be laid out both inside and outside, in a variety of materials and different designs. For simplicity, the classical design is easiest, but a pattern modelled on the Chartres style, although more time-consuming to construct, can be more rewarding to walk. (See the Appendix for instructions on designing simple labyrinths.) In some instances, particularly with outdoor labyrinths, the construction of the labyrinth can become part of the workshop or worship event itself.

Other types of labyrinth

There will be occasions when space is restricted, and floor-size labyrinths not available. Equally, the members of a workshop or worship event may not find it easy to walk the distances involved or to keep their balance while negotiating the curves and twists of the labyrinth pattern. In these situations, a finger labyrinth can be a reliable alternative. Labyrinth patterns can be downloaded from the internet – a good, copyright-free source is Wiki-media Commons (common.wikimedia.org). You will find here both classic and Chartres-style designs which can be printed off in an appropriate size. If they are then laminated, these labyrinths can be traced with the finger or with a washable marker pen. Finger labyrinths can be used not only on those occasions when a floor labyrinth is too difficult or space is too restricted, but as a way of introducing the concept of the labyrinth at the beginning of a workshop. An A4-size pattern that can be held in the hand will give a good impression of the nature of the labyrinth, whereas simply looking at a full-size one may be confusing or threatening. This is a particularly useful exercise when working with the elderly, children and other vulnerable groups. Sturdier versions of a finger labyrinth can be made out of wood, clay or pewter, and can be purchased online through outlets such as Veriditas. The UK-based Pilgrim Paths (www.pilgrimpaths.co.uk) sells quilted fabric labyrinths as well as wooden finger labyrinths and small postcard-labyrinth designs.

For walking the labyrinth without following a visible path, labyrinth beads are invaluable. Small enough to be kept in a pocket, these beads can be used as the basis for a labyrinth walk without following a path, in any location of whatever size. Instructions for making a set of beads can be found in the Appendix.

Online labyrinths

Alternatively, there are a number of websites offering an online labyrinth experience. The Labyrinth Society (www.labyrinthsociety.org) offers an online labyrinth experience, as does the reJesus site (www.rejesus.co.uk). These provide good online introductions to labyrinth spirituality, although some might find the lack of physical engagement disconcerting. Labyrinth (www.labyrinth. org.uk) also offers a useful insight into labyrinths as spiritual tools.

For a broader look at labyrinths, the main sites are those belonging to Veriditas (www.veriditas.org), the Labyrinth Society (www.labyrinthsociety.org) and Labyrinthos (www.labyrinthos.net). Following the links from these main sites should enable the diligent researcher to discover almost everything they need to know!

Books

The following list of books, although not exhaustive, provides a useful basis for a labyrinth library:

Artress, L. (1995), *Walking a Sacred Path*, New York: Riverhead.

Attali, J. (1999), *The Labyrinth in Culture and Society*, Berkeley: North Atlantic Books.

Geoffrion, J. K. H. (2004), *Christian Prayer and Labyrinth*, Cleveland: Pilgrim Press.

Geoffrion, J. K. H. (1999), *Praying the Labyrinth*, Cleveland: Pilgrim Press.

Jaskolski, H. (1997), *The Labyrinth: Symbol of Fear, Rebirth and Liberation*, London: Shambala.

MacQueen, G. (2005), *The Spirituality of Mazes and Labyrinths*, Kelowna: Northstone.

Sewell, R., Sellers, J. and Williams, D. (2012), *Working with the Labyrinth: Paths for Exploration*, Iona: Wild Goose.

Tarrant, I. and Dakin, S. (2004), *Labyrinths and Prayer Stations*, Cambridge: Grove.

Telesco, P. (2001), *Labyrinth Walking: Patterns of Power*, New York: Kensington.

Welch, S. (2011), *Walking the Labyrinth*, Norwich: Canterbury Press.

Williams, D. (2011), *Labyrinth: Landscape of the Soul*, Iona: Wild Goose.

Wright, C. (2004), *The Maze and the Warrior*, Cambridge, Mass.: Harvard University Press.

Sacred space

Davies, D. (1994), *Christianity from Sacred Place*, ed. Jean Holm, London: Cassell.

Giles, R. (1996), *Repitching the Tent*, Norwich: Canterbury Press.

Holm, J. and Bowker, J. (1994), *Sacred Place*, London: Pinter.

Inge, J. A. (2003), *A Christian Theology of Place*, Aldershot: Ashgate.

Sheldrake, P. (2001), *Spaces for the Sacred*, Norwich: Canterbury Press.

Appendix

Creating a Labyrinth

Fuller instructions can be found in *Walking the Labyrinth* by Sally Welch – this is intended as a brief guide only.

Constructing a Chartres-style labyrinth

This guide is for the simplest and most straightforward of the labyrinth designs. Petals may be added to the central circle and lunation around the outside: for an example see *Walking the Labyrinth*, page 65.

Equipment

To draw the Chartres-style pattern you need to set aside at least two hours, probably three. You will also need some volunteers to help, lots of reels of masking tape, coloured self-adhesive dots and a good pair of compasses. This needs to be weighted so that it does not move. I have made mine using one end of a set of hand weights with a length of rope looped over the rod. The rope needs to be able to move in 360° very freely and should be longer than the diameter of your labyrinth. The weight needs to be heavy enough not to move – do not be tempted to ask a volunteer merely to hold the rope as the slightest movement on their part will make a serious distortion to the pattern.

If you are making the labyrinth outside, use the paint that is used to mark out tennis courts – if you can obtain the use of the marking machine itself, that will make things very much easier.

When using masking tape inside, I have always gone round on my hands and knees, but Robert Ferré's website (www.labyrinth-enterprises.com) has instructions for a homemade masking tape dispenser which may make things easier.

Initial calculations

The given figure is that the centre is a quarter of the diameter of the whole of the labyrinth and that the path is 14"/36cm wide, allowing for a 2"/5cm wide masking tape or paint 'wall'. For a labyrinth of 11 circuits with a centre of approximately 9'/2.75m, the diameter of the whole will be 34½'/13.25m.

Eleven-circuit labyrinth

The first thing to do is mark off on your compass where the 12 lines that make up the walls of the labyrinth will be. Place the compass in the centre of your site and do not move it from there again. The first measurement is for the centre which is 9'/2.75m (or 108"/275cm) in diameter. However, since the compass is in the centre of this the measurement needs to be only half. Accordingly, make a mark on the rope 54"/137cm along the rope. For the next 11 lines, simply add 14"/36cm to each measurement:

Line 1   54"/137cm
Line 2   68"/173cm
Line 3   82"/208cm
Line 4   96"/244cm
Line 5   110"/279cm
Line 6   124"/315cm
Line 7   138"/351cm
Line 8   152"/386cm
Line 9   166"/422cm
Line 10   180"/475cm
Line 11   194"/493cm
Line 12   208"/528cm

Before you start to make the circles that form the outlines of the paths, mark the two straight entry paths that go from the centre of the labyrinth to the outside. Decide first where you want the entrance to be, taking into consideration those factors discussed in Chapter 3. Line the compass rope up to where you need the entrance and mark the path with the rope in the middle. That is, ensure 7"/18cm either side of the rope and tape a line each side. Then measure 14"/36cm to the left of that path and tape a line there. Parts of this will be removed later, but the entrance is at least in place. The tape lines of the path do not need to go into the centre, so begin the line at the first marker on your compass.

Once your entrance paths are in place, move the compass rope around the diameter of the circle, getting your helpers to place sticky dots or pieces of masking tape on the floor where the paths will go. The more helpers you have – about six is best – the quicker this process will be. Remember to hold the compass rope at the same tautness each time or otherwise distortions will occur. This is a lengthy process, but if you make the gaps between dots too far apart it will be harder to get the path width consistent when joining the dots with tape.

When you have marked the floor all the way around, join the dots with masking tape. Although this is fairly flexible, it will not lie flat as you are taping in a circle. Do not worry overmuch about this; it will fold and tuck where it needs to. Simply keep pressing the tape down as you go to avoid sharp angles.

Your labyrinth will now have 11 concentric circles and 2 straight paths into a centre.

The turns must now be put in, by using strips of masking tape across pairs of path to form a cross design. It helps if you mark 'North', 'East', 'West' and 'South' on the floor ('South' is the entrance path).

At the top arm of the cross, pointing North, tape the first three lines together, starting with the outside line. Then leave a path blank and tape the next three lines together. Leave a path blank and tape the next three lines together. Leave a path blank and tape the final three lines together.

At the end of the left arm of the cross, pointing West, miss the first path then tape the next three lines together. Miss one path, then tape the next three lines; miss one path and tape the next three lines, leaving two paths blank before the centre.

At the end of the right arm of the cross, pointing East, miss the first two paths, then tape three lines together. Miss a path, and tape three lines together, miss a path and tape three lines together, leaving one path blank before the centre.

At each piece of cross tape, remove 12"/30cm of wall tape either side of the cross tape. This forms the turn.

For the entrance paths, take the left-hand piece of tape first. Remove 12"/30cm of tape from the walls of the labyrinth numbered 11, 9, 5 and 3 (counting the outside wall as 12) as they approach the entrance tape.

Then remove 12"/30cm of entrance tape at paths 7, 6 and 1 (counting the outside path as 11).

Continue wall 7 across the entrance path.

For the right-hand entrance path, take the right-hand piece of tape. Remove 12"/30cm of tape from walls 10, 8, 4 and 2.

Remove 12"/30cm of tape from entrance tape at paths 11, 6 and 5.

Continue walls 12 and 6 across the right-hand entrance path.

You now have a simple 11-circuit Chartres-style labyrinth.

Seven-circuit labyrinth

If you want a smaller labyrinth, a 7-circuit one can be made with a diameter of about 24'/7.3m. This assumes that the 9'/2.75m diameter centre circle is kept the same. The construction method is also the same, but drawing only 8 lines, beginning with one 54"/1.4m from the centre and then adding 14"/36cm until you reach 152"/386cm.

If you want to drop down to 22'/6.7m, the best way is to make the centre 5'/1.5m in diameter. The measurements would then be:

Line 1	30"/76cm
Line 2	44"/112cm
Line 3	58"/147cm
Line 4	72"/183cm
Line 5	86"/218cm
Line 6	100"/254cm
Line 7	114"/297cm
Line 8	128"/325cm

In both cases, continue with the construction method for the 11-circuit labyrinth until you reach the section on making the turns.

Again, it helps if you mark 'North', 'East', 'West' and 'South' on the floor ('South' is the entrance path).

At the top arm of the cross (pointing North), tape the first three lines together, starting with the outside line. Then leave a path blank and tape the next three lines together. Leave the final two paths blank.

At the left arm (West), miss the first path then tape the next three lines together. Miss a path then tape the next three lines, leaving the final path blank.

At the right arm (East), miss the first two paths, tape

the next three lines, miss a path, than tape the next three lines.

At each piece of cross tape, remove 12″/31cm of wall tape from either side of the cross tape. This forms the turn.

For the entrance paths, take the left-hand piece of tape first. Remove 12″/31cm of tape from walls 7, 5 and 2 (counting the outside wall as 8) of the labyrinth as they approach the entrance tape.

Then remove 12"/31cm of entrance tape at paths 3, 2 and 1 (counting the outside path as 7).

Continue walls 3 and 1 across the entrance path.

For the right-hand entrance path, take the right-hand piece of tape. Remove 12"/31cm of tape from walls 6 and 4.

Remove 12"/31cm of tape from the entrance tape at paths 7, 2 and 1.

Continue walls 8 and 2 across the right-hand entrance path.

Building a Classical-style labyrinth

1 Begin by drawing a cross in the centre of your space.

2 In the path of a circle, place four dots midway between the arms of the cross. You can draw the circle by placing a stick with a rope attached in the middle of the cross, like a giant pair of compasses.

3 The centre of the labyrinth is made by drawing an arc to connect the top arm of the cross with the dot to the right. To do this accurately, find the midpoint between arm and dot, and using your 'compasses' connect the two.

4 The dot to the left of the top arm of the cross is then joined to the right-hand arm of the cross, sweeping round above the centre.

5 The left arm of the cross is then joined to the dot below the right arm of the cross.

6 Finally, the bottom left-hand dot is joined to the bottom arm of the cross.

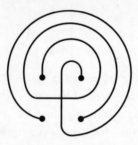

7 To increase the number of circuits, more details are added to the seed pattern, but the principle remains the same – join the top arm of the cross to the point nearest to it on the right. Moving systematically, join the next point on the left to the next point on the right until the pattern is complete.

A virtual Chartres-style labyrinth

At its simplest, the pathway of the Chartres labyrinth is nothing more than turns to different compass points either towards a centre point or away from it. A Chartres labyrinth can be walked around a centre point without the help of walls or paths, simply using compass points or beads as a guide.

To begin with, mark the centre point of your labyrinth with something, then mark or note the position of the four points of the compass. I always make my entrance at the south because it is easier to hold the other compass points in my head like that. Imagine a cross extending to these four points across the centre.

Marking the entrance sequence is simple. Walk south from the centre as far as you can, then walk north half-way back to the centre.

N

W   ×   E

↑
S

Walk west in an arc to the imaginary arm of the cross that stretches east to west. This is indicated in the diagram as W:

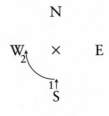

N

W   ×   E

S

Then turn towards the centre and walk back to the north–
south arm of the cross. This is indicated by a lower-case
letter because we are turning towards the centre, and the
compass direction in which we are moving – south.

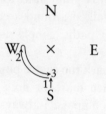

Walk towards the centre again as you did at the beginning – north.

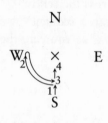

After the entrance sequence, continue walking towards
the arm of the cross indicated by each compass direction.
If the letter is a capital, turn away from the centre; if it is
lower case, turn towards the centre.

Entrance sequence (from S):

   x paces N
   W
   s
   x paces N
   wn
   WS

W
S
WN
w
ne
n
es
E
S
EN
E
NW
N
WS
W
S
WN
w
ne
n
es
E
S
EN
ES

Centre sequence (from S):

x paces N
E
s
x paces N

Labyrinth beads

As a list of compass points, the virtual labyrinth is easy to work out, but not so easy to remember. A useful tool for walking the labyrinth without any visual help is to convert the compass directions to objects – a set of beads works wonderfully well.

First, find eight different types of bead. It makes it easier if you have one type of bead, for example, plain glass, that can be obtained in two sizes and four colours. So an ideal would be large and small red, green, blue and yellow beads, for example.

Each colour represents a compass direction – Red for South, Green for West, Blue for North, and Yellow for East. Small beads represent a turn towards the centre, large beads a turn away from it. Simply thread the beads according to the compass points above.

The beginning of the string is marked with a cross. This represents the entrance and centre series. The entrance series takes you up the left side of the cross (4 paces N, turn to the west; turn to the south, then 4 paces N). The centre series takes you up the right side of the cross (4 paces N, turn to the east; turn to the south, then 4 paces N). The journey begins and ends at the cross.

These beads can be taken anywhere and the labyrinth walked at any time in any space.